A BOOKSELLER'S WAR

A BOOKSELLER'S WAR

HEYWOOD AND ANNE HILL

EDITED BY
JONATHAN GATHORNE-HARDY

MICHAEL RUSSELL

© individual correspondents 1997
Editorial matter © Jonathan Gathorne-Hardy 1997

First published in Great Britain 1997
by Michael Russell (Publishing) Ltd
Wilby Hall, Wilby, Norwich NR16 2JP

Typeset in Sabon by The Typesetting Bureau
Allen House, East Borough, Wimborne, Dorset
Printed and bound in Great Britain
by Biddles Ltd, Guildford and King's Lynn

ISBN 0 85955 237 3

Contents

Introduction

During the months before Heywood had started his bookshop I was quite delighted at the prospect of working in it, and was impatient to begin; but as the time grew near I began to be apprehensive. Despite having just completed a Pitman's course of typing and double-entry book-keeping I found it hard to believe I would really be able to do what was necessary in a sufficiently effective and reliable way. Shy, and rather deficient in presence of mind, how would I cope with the customers? Perhaps lots coming in at once, perhaps in Heywood's lunch hour when I was alone in the shop? The thought of having to say 'Heywood Hill' down the telephone for some reason embarrassed me, and I dreaded having to do it. A more serious worry was that I might get into muddles with the accounts and find myself getting behind-hand with everything, perhaps seriously 'letting Heywood down'. Perhaps even ruining him by some colossal accounting error.

The shop opened on 3 August 1936 at No. 17 Curzon Street. We didn't have a party for this, but instead had one a little later for a book by Oliver Messel. It was a success: we sold satisfactory numbers of the book, and people were clearly impressed by the beauty of the shop and the glories of its stock – which included pictures, prints and other objects that Heywood liked, including musical boxes. Buying things and looking at them afterwards was a source of great pleasure and for him one of the important points of the shop.

After about a week I found that, except in the case of occasional individuals, coping with customers had not proved difficult. The relationship between them and us was, of course, a simple and straightforward one: they wanted to buy books, we wanted to sell them. I quickly learnt that some people needed possibly quite a lot of help and advice, whereas others just wanted to be left to look around on their own, sometimes for ages, without being distracted or irritated by being spoken to at all; and there was every possible variation between those extremes.

One of the pleasures of relations with customers was that I found I really liked quite a number of them; some became real friends, occasionally for the rest of my life (or of theirs). Yet the obverse of this was also true: some customers were difficult, perhaps demanding, or rude or painfully boring. (The bores were often the longest staying, as well as causing us the most suffering.) But, we agreed, we must be stoical about this; the difficult customers weren't after all very numerous. Heywood had had seven years' practice at that and at everything else to do with bookselling; I had everything to learn. I was determined to become truly professional – it would be amateurish to be ruffled by customers' behaviour, and that at least I could avoid. But, as will be seen later, there were occasions when I didn't avoid it.

The most important point of working in a bookshop is the most totally obvious one – that what is being sold is not, say, fish or meat or shoes, but books. The fact that publishers gave proof copies of new books to booksellers was a delightful surprise to me. My shelves to this day abound in them, in tattered condition, vintage '30s to '60s. And we allowed ourselves to take home and read books from stock too; but only with the greatest possible caution and care, dust-jackets removed and put in a place of safety, hands scrupulously clean, no reading at meals.

Having hitherto been always and only a buyer, suddenly to be a seller too made me, when I shopped, observe with interest, critical or appreciative, the way other sellers behaved. Sometimes abominably, I found; but there were others who truly impressed me, and indeed helped me; I occasionally copied their techniques with customers.

My worries over whether I would be able to cope with the book-keeping having to be done not just in class, but in a real shop, were found to be baseless. After a day or two it all turned out to be much simpler than I expected, and there had been no setbacks. I was quite proud of the neatly typed letters and bills I sent out, and interested in discovering what our better or more interesting customers had bought. It was a huge relief to me that there wasn't too much work, as I had feared there might be. I was not a fast worker (far from it) but was keeping pace with things quite successfully. I was to discover later that this was only because we hadn't got nearly enough customers. In fact, the sales for 1936–7 were £3,644, and the loss (no question of profits) was £240. In 1937–8 the sales were £3,736, and the loss £314.

We – I say 'we' because I had bought a £1 share in the shop just before it started and regarded this as entitling me to speak of the shop as 'ours', and decisions made solely by Heywood as being 'ours' too; so – *we* were not too worried about the repeated losses, as friends in the trade who had warned Heywood that they thought success was improbable also said that even if the shop should succeed, we must expect to make a loss for five years – which as it turned out was exactly what happened. Our perpetually pressing problem for many years was whether the sales would produce enough cash to pay the shop's many expenses, including our wages, and this was often touch and go. What saved us ultimately was the rationing of nearly everything but books.

No. 17 was not unlike No. 10 where the shop is now, but more spacious. It had no shop front, but two large sash windows; and as at No. 10 you went up some steps and left into two big rooms: Heywood's the red room, mine at the back painted white.

At first Heywood actually lived in the shop – sleeping on a double bed in the far left-hand corner of the white room. During the day it had a mustard-coloured cover. On the far right a door led to the bathroom, big enough for a chest-of-drawers, a wardrobe, some chairs and a little cooker. Downstairs was a basement, large but damp and undecorated, where Jim McKillop packed the books, delivering then on a bicycle with a big basket saying G. HEYWOOD HILL LTD – BOOKSELLER on it. (I lived in a bedsitter at this time, from which I bicycled to work.)

Finding I could manage, I was elated and jubilant. I sat at my small, modern, white desk (designed by John Hill), sometimes for quite a long time, not working but gazing in recurrent wonder at the vista of the two interconnecting rooms: my white, larger one, lined with the multi-coloured dust-jacketed new books; beyond it, near the entrance, the red room where Heywood could just be seen in the extreme distance facing me at his antique desk with his back to the window, with mostly leather-bound old books in carved wooden shelves reaching nearly to the ceiling all round the room. I could catch glimpses of one or two of his extraordinary collection of early musical boxes: most were not boxes at all, but monkeys, ballet-dancers, clergymen, sailors, drummer-boys, judges or ships,

[9]

all moving in appropriate ways, either when the clock struck or when a button was pressed.

A train of thought could start on these occasions, semi-paralysing me as far as work was concerned. One recurrent thought was: this is the most remarkable shop and I am very lucky to be in at the beginning of it. Then I would speculate about the future. What would have happened to it by next year, the year after, or in five, ten or fifteen years hence? (More than fifteen years was too distant to contemplate.) Not knowing, I decided, made the whole thing as exciting as the start of an expedition to some unknown part of the world.

I thought too how extraordinarily lucky it was that I liked Heywood so much. But on the other hand what a waste it was, when the conditions were so propitious, that we were not in love.

All these things were to change – changes which are the substance of what follows.

ANNE HILL

Beginnings

Anne Gathorne-Hardy and I opened my bookshop on 3 August 1936 at No. 17 Curzon Street (it was moved seven years later to No. 10). For this my father had lent me £2,000 – a kind action on his part, especially as he had earlier started me off in a stock-broker's office where I had been useless.

A not very encouraging event, which had preceded the opening by only a few months, had been the going bust of the antiquarian book-shop Elkin Mathews after fifty years' trading, and where Anne's brother Eddie had worked since about 1925. Most friends in the book trade tended, too, to prophesy disaster. Not enough capital, they said. And it was the middle of the Great Depression.

However, we were not put off by all this. I, who had been working for seven years in another antiquarian bookshop (Chas. J. Sawyer's), was delighted to be starting on my own.

To begin with there was just us and a book-packer/delivery boy, Jim McKillop. We ran the place on a shoestring, paying ourselves a small weekly wage (Anne £2. 10/-; me £5). I had been in Paris and Vienna to buy stock, Anne to a typing and book-keeping school. In many ways, those early years were the happiest. We were so to speak on trial with one another as well as in the running of a small busi-ness. By great luck both trials worked. We married after about a year.

The war came, and a point was reached when it looked as if the business might founder. The two young men who had replaced Anne when we got married, Peter Yates and Geoffrey Larkin, were called up in the early months, so she came back. Soon after, Nancy Mitford joined us. I was called up in November 1942. We filled in forms asking for a temporary reprieve, on the grounds that one third of the shop's sales took place in December. (The shop was technically a 'one-man business', despite the fact that four people, two of them women, worked there.)

No reply came, so I left for the Army – only to be met by orders that I should return at once, since mine was a one-man business at risk. I duly did so but was called up again on 17 December. Anne was by now four months pregnant. However, by then Nancy had been in the shop for about a year. Despite her wit and apparent frivolity she was a hard worker, and a friend, so when I left I knew that Anne would have effective help.

I had not been a bad bookseller but was an utterly rotten soldier. How very rotten can be seen in my letters to Anne. We only decided to publish this correspondence because we think that my catastrophes in the Army and Anne's in the shop are sometimes quite funny.

In December 1942 I was thirty-six, Anne thirty-one.

HEYWOOD HILL

This was written in 1984. Heywood died in April 1986, three months before his eightieth birthday.

Maidstone, 1942

Thursday, 17 December 1942
I went very early to Heywood Hill's shop to buy Christmas cards; and happened to arrive just as poor Heywood was about to go off to the Army, for he has at last been called up. Anne very miserable and unnaturally cheerful. She is to have a baby in May. Heywood slunk off sadly and infinitely quietly, as is his wont, Anne trying to be brave. I meant to appear unconscious of the true situation, and chatted away brutally; then left as soon as possible.

JAMES LEES MILNE, *Ancestral Voices*

From ANNE
10 Warwick Avenue
London W.2
Friday, 18 December (finished 20th) 9 p.m.

Darling Heywood,

Been having the most wildly hectic two days. I didn't start to write yesterday as I was in unutterable misery and sobbing despair over a shop event (which turned out not to matter).

There have been streams and streams of people almost unendingly, 10 and 12 and 20 at once, and sales large with good big things in them. Nancy has been very wonderful, and she and not me has sold nearly all the most expensive things. *Latham's Birds* for £21,[1] and two things Mr Merino[2] bought in yesterday for £9 she sold today, one to Lord Dundonald for a present for Lady Anderson, and the other to Violet Trefusis; the two I think fetched £15. Merino was very pleased when we paid him today.

I wonder if all this seems very painful and remote for you to read

1 *Latham's Birds* would now be worth about £1,200.
2 Mr Merino was a 'runner', someone who goes from bookshop to bookshop, buying books and selling them for resale. He sometimes left books of his own in the shop on sale or return .

about. It has been for me most emotional and also agitating in the shop, with you not being there; and important shop events seemed to take place all the time. Yesterday Harry[3] rang up at about 11, and wanted us to bid for him at Sotheby's, lots 245-55, which Nancy worked out would start about half past one. After hesitation I said we would. Then today it was nearly twelve and there were about 15 people in the shop, and one of them turned out to be the person to fit me for my maternity belt,[4] and I had to go to the bathroom and be stark naked being measured for about half an hour. When I came out there were still about 15 people, amongst them Antony and Ruth and Sammy, and Jonny[5] beating a tom-tom. Nancy rang up Sotheby's at about half past twelve, to find out how the lots were going, and discovered that the first 200 things in the catalogue had all been withdrawn, and all the lots Harry wanted had been sold. This was rather dreadful, and upset me, as I felt we were failing him the moment you left; but to make up in the afternoon the British Museum rang up to say they're buying his MS, isn't it splendid? He's never rung up so he doesn't know any of all this yet.

I don't remember much about the afternoon, but the really shattering thing happened when I was tidying my desk at about 7.30. I suddenly found on it a printed sheet of paper about the Merchant Navy Comforts Fund Sale thing, that Raymond[6] had been collecting all those books for; it said that they must be delivered on the 16th and 17th, and that the sale ended yesterday at 9.30. This really nearly killed me. Raymond had brought in lots more books, Harold Nicolson, Vita Sackville-West, William Beveridge,[7] Cecil Beaton, and about five others, and he's got them all to autograph them. I put them all in a basket and rushed out into the rain, leaving the shop unlocked and my diamond star brooch in the bathroom, and everything all over the floor. I got a taxi in Shepherd's Market and went to the Mayfair, and it was the worst kind of nightmare, the enormous ballroom crowded and packed with beastly people, and tables with horrible women sitting at them, and I blundered

3 Harry Clifton, a good customer, eccentric. He used to give orders for strange tasks to be undertaken, and objects to be bought, unconnected with bookselling.
4 A sort of corset pregnant women were supposed to wear then.
5 Gathorne-Hardy (see Appendix).
6 Raymond Mortimer, writer and critic and for many years chief reviewer of *The Sunday Times*.
7 The Beveridge Report had been published in February.

with my bundle of books from table to table stammering. Everybody said I was much too late and there was nothing to be done. They were all quite odious. I went home crying hard in the taxi, with the awful task ahead of me of having to tell Raymond. I rang up Nancy and blubbed down the telephone to her; she was extremely nice, and reassured me slightly by saying that Raymond had come in that afternoon with more books, which I hadn't known, and that it was *his* fault. But it didn't really help much. I rang up Hester[8] for Raymond's number, and told her, and she was appalled on my behalf, and said 'I *do* pity you', but that it must be an anodyne against minding you being gone so much, like Ronnie's leg being so bad made her forget about her mother being dead. I said your being gone made me mind 20 times more, as if you were here *you'd* have to tell Raymond and not me. He was out when I did ring; but I tried again this morning after breakfast and told him, and he couldn't possibly have been more extremely nice – he said that he had definitely been told the sale was on Saturday, and had told all the authors it was Saturday, so it was not our fault in the least. I had thought that my conviction that the sale was Saturday, and that delivering them on Friday would be all right, must have been just a private delusion of my own. He said to keep quiet about it all, and not to tell the authors or make a fuss about it. It must have been most annoying for him really; he had been so pleased at having got William Beveridge to sign, and so altogether pleased at having collected so many, I thought he was really splendid about it, even thinking it was funny in a way. The relief about this made me feel elated, and I went to the shop this morning in a very good mood, better than I ever could have believed possible. I tidied a good deal, and filled the empty places on the tables with things from the shelves.

Today has been a roaring rush, but everything I think is fairly under control. Though I feel I may very easily have put wrong labels on books and sent letters to wrong addresses. There are a lot of tiresome letters saying books haven't arrived and people haven't been thanked yet. My brain gets to reel and whirl with shop things. It will be wonderful to be at Snape.[9] If only to God you could be there too though.

A man came in today, whom I recognised vaguely but couldn't

8 Hester Griffin (see Appendix).
9 Snape Priory, Saxmundham, Suffolk. The home of Anne's mother, Dorothy Cranbrook (see Appendix).

remember who he was. He was rather nice, very appreciative about the shop and bought about £8. 10/-[10] worth of things (not old books but lots of them duds we didn't think would ever sell, and not off the tables but off the shelves). Also an entire set of Proust. When he wrote his cheque I saw he was Peter Glenville, and then had to say about his old account. I feel I did it clumsily, and he was rather appalled, obviously didn't remember it in the least. He paid, and was quite nice, but I felt I had slightly dished the relationship I had established between us while selling things to him and advising about presents.

To people who ring up asking if we're open on Saturday afternoon I have said yes, between 3 and 5. Nancy has now volunteered to stay in the afternoon instead of me, and I am slightly contemplating letting her, dreadful though it will be not clearing things as I should. I will make the Smiths[11] bring back the day book and ledgers so that I can enter over the weekend. They have been quite good; Smith mended the blackout in the packing room and stayed till about quarter past seven tonight.

The Lambes[12] have asked me to a concert on Sunday afternoon but I said no. Too much to do. Also am sure I should sleep at it. I am having lunch with them, and really shall probably sleep at home after it and not do anything. Rather awful in one way, as I would have gone to Norway,[13] and now probably shan't till after Christmas, when it will have been a very long time and she will probably scold me and turn me out.

A rather strange ironic thing has been that Tony's[14] husband arrived back from the Middle East yesterday, and while I was crying alone in the sitting-room, the house was ringing with the sounds of merry de Sarigny reunion. The hall is full of his Middle East tin trunks. I haven't seen him yet.

I do long intensely to get a letter from you. I feel it almost can't

10 'Old' money: £1 = 20 shillings (20/-); 1 shilling (1/-) = 12 pence (12d); 2/6 (two shillings and sixpence) was half-a-crown.
11 A couple who worked for Anne's and Heywood's neighbour Lord Kinross, who lived at 6 Warwick Avenue. The husband and son worked in the shop.
12 Charles and Peta Lambe (see Appendix).
13 'Norway' was a small restaurant in Warwick Place. Mrs Rusted, the fat, eccentric and finally mad proprietress, was Norwegian, the restaurant nameless, so Norway was used for both.
14 Tony de Sarigny (a girl) was the Hills' tenant, and lived on their top floor. Her husband was away at the war except when home on leave.

fail to be dreadfully horrible, bleak and alarming; but I want to know what it *is* like.

Saturday 19 December [same letter]
Just back from what turned out to be rather a distinguished little lunch at Ivy [Compton-Burnett]'s – Rose Macaulay, Ernest Thesiger and me the only guests. I am to clique[15] a book for Rose Macaulay (*Scandals and Cruelties of John Aubrey*) and she says she's coming to see the shop; I am terrified of not recognising her if she does. I was rather impressed by her. Very sensitive and distinguished-looking. I can't remember anything that was said by anyone. I had hoped beforehand that at last I might be able to because of writing to you. We were all given Christmas presents on leaving of a small tin of black-currant purée each.

I walked back up Kensington Church Street, and am now regretting I didn't buy a rather pretty Victorian partly coloured drawing of a child holding a cat in a doorway, framed, for £1. I was trying to be cautious and thought it expensive, but now I don't; I feel sure in the next few days we'd have sold it for 35/- or £2. All I did buy all the way up Church Street was *Swiss Family Robinson* with coloured plates for 3/- (which Mrs Goldsmith wants) and *Anna Karenina* in French for 3/6.

Now I'm going to wash my hair. I fear this letter is much too long and garrulous and may be embarrassing for you to read in public somehow, so many pages, but it is such a pleasure to write to you (not at all a task like you said) that I cannot help going on and on.

Love from
ANNE

From OSBERT SITWELL

Renishaw Hall
Renishaw
Nr Sheffield
Friday 18 December

My dear Anne,
I have been thinking so much of you in the last week. I tried to ring you up on Wednesday, both at the shop and at home, but you

15 *The Clique* was a weekly paper where booksellers advertised for old and out-of-print books they wanted. They also read it in case they had any of the books that were being advertised for. To 'clique' a book meant to advertise it in this way.

were out when I got on eventually. I only wanted to find out if Heywood had had a reprieve, but I gathered not from your maid[16] (who seemed very nice).

I think you must both of you know how keenly I feel for you in all this beastliness and breaking up. I think being parted from people one likes is *intolerable* and there is little comfort I can offer, except that I am sure you will shine as a buyer of books and come out of that triumphantly. I told Heywood so. I don't believe you'll mind the extra work a bit. And, for the rest, if I was a betting man, I'd lay odds that H. is out of it by June next. I am hoping for a mild attack of bronchial pneumonia for him – it's not much to ask and I've only just escaped it – if I have – myself.

However, this letter is only to carry you my affection – and let me know if I can do anything for H. Would he like letters – and if so what is his degrading address?

I've been reading through my autobiography – it's the only book I've ever been pleased with, that I wrote – but goodness knows when it can come out.[17] I have no news, which makes a dull letter.

Yours ever,
OSBERT

From HEYWOOD

2 Platoon, C Coy
GSC, 13th of TC
Invicta Lines
Maidstone
18 December 1942

Darling, darling Anne,

I'm confused and bewildered, still. Shall just blunderingly try to tell you what's happening to me. Even more people. Mostly youths. I was inoculated – then put in a squad of about 7 of the older people. Then marched to where they give out uniforms. One was given a kitbag, and thousands of things were poured into it. Measured like lightning and given overcoat and uniform – all stuffed in the kitbag except the overcoat, and we had to carry the kitbag and overcoat and hand-bag a long way. It was too heavy for me and fell off and I simply couldn't, so the corporal had to carry it

16 Mrs Sternson (see Appendix).
17 *Left Hand: Right Hand*. The book couldn't be published while his father was still alive.

[18]

(first failure), but I did carry someone else's hand-bag and overcoat, and that fell in the mud.

Then a meal in a huge hall, just the 7 of us. Mincemeat, but couldn't eat much of it. Quite nice the others, but impossible to speak much. Then separated from them and into my tent. Almost 40 people. Beds sort of wooden trestles six inches apart. Palliasses with the straw coming out, and a straw pillow. The light is very bad and I can't see well. Shrieking wireless (The Western Bros). An awful job stowing one's things in a tiny locker, but youths came and helped, but then one doesn't know where anything is – it all has to be folded in a special way. There's a rather slick young man in the next bed who's already making friends with the sergeant.

Then there was tea, which was exactly like a scene in one of those gaol films. The whole enormous room filled with a sort of shouting fury. There was a fight about food opposite me.

Now I've been in the hut for a long time and am in a sort of stupor. I ought to have brought some paper and string to post my clothes back, but may be able to get some from somewhere. I've lost some vital buttons for the sort of dungarees, but expect that will be all right. The sergeant has just announced we get up tomorrow at ¼ past 6, and that there won't be much more than lectures and dental inspections till Monday, when he says the Programme will begin.

There's quite a nice bald-headed man on the other side of me; I told him I was in a muddle and he laughed. I dropped my blankets in the mud. I think I've brought too many little things. I see nobody yet to be really matey with, but it's too early.

I must go on fiddling about with my things.

Please, please don't work yourself too hard at the shop and if you haven't finished just force yourself to stop. There are such wonderful excuses.

We're going to be allowed out to the NAAFI soon. Not out of the camp for seven days I gather from talk.

The wireless has stopped now. Nobody notices one much which is nice, it's like one of those Ackermann prints of Bedlam. The wireless has begun again.

Love my darling,
HEYWOOD

Saturday, 19 December, about 5 p.m.

Darling Heywood,

Lovely to get your letter. It does all sound awful though; what misery, misery.

I have missed you very much today. At breakfast especially for some reason, which I also used to find particularly poignant in the days before you left. Though one never realised it, they were so very agreeable. Your breakfasts and mornings, with the getting up in a hurry and scurry, must be horribly awful. Oh dear. Perhaps though you will be back this time six weeks, and living at home. It's possible; it does happen to some people.

All is still well at the shop. Viva[18] came, and I gave her her present as she was leaving. We're still selling lots of little objects and pictures; both the silhouettes, the little oval embroidered flower picture, two scrap-books, several maple-framed pictures, and possibly the frosted glass snake vase. Peter Glenville came in again and bought more, so that was all right. Harry has been told about everything, and doesn't seem to mind about the Sotheby things. But he wants a letter from the British Museum, praising the special picture in the MS, and thanking him for it's being so cheap! The wonderful thing is he's going to get one, as I knew Aunty Wormald[19] was coming in this afternoon, and told Nancy to tell him all about Harry if there was a chance, and to ask him if it would be possible. Now I've just rung her up, and it was all a great success she says, and he *is* going to write to Harry.

I didn't go back this afternoon. It was rather awful shutting the shop for lunch and I felt very guilty, but I put up the notice saying 'Open between 3 & 5'.

Sunday, (20th), 11.30 a.m. in bed

I must finish now so that I can post this on the way to the Lambes.

I've left my list of shop queries in the shop of course, but don't think there was anything very vitally vital. The chief mystery has been a telegram, unsigned, from Cold Ash near Newbury, saying send *Barchester Towers* to a certain address, and 'the remaining

18 Viva (Dorothy) King, wife of Willie King (see later). Her autobiography *The Weeping and the Laughter* was published in 1976.
19 Francis Wormald, author and art critic; lived with his wife Honoria in London and the West Country.

volumes' to Cold Ash. I simply cannot remember who lives at Cold Ash, but the Post Office is enquiring. We've only about 3 extremely shabby Trollopes left to send to whoever it is.

It was lovely speaking to you last night; do try again; I'm in every night.

Jim [McKillop][20] rang up last night and was very sweet and touching. All his news I expect will be in his letter, so I shan't write about it.

I must get up now.

Fondest love, darling Heywood, from your devoted loving

ANNE

From HEYWOOD   Maidstone
                                                  Saturday 19 December 1942
Darling Anne,

I can see it's going to be fairly grim here and I'm going to write you gloomy letters, and spare you nothing – like we said. It's a perpetual agitation of tiny things – of buttons that won't undo and things to fold in a particular way. I've found no beginnings of a buddy and am awfully dumb. There's a kindly man in the next bed who helps me fold things, but he's got a particular mate of his own on his other side. The one who was on my other side has got two weeks off because his wife's had twins. The competence of the others at polishing etc. makes me feel awfully clumsy and stupid. Nearly all the men in my hut are in their thirties which is a good thing, and all fairly gloomy. Today has seemed very long. Nobody slept much. A bugle went at ¼ past 6 (I hadn't put on pyjamas as nobody else did). There's a scramble into the wash place, and such a crowd. You can't get a basin. Cold water (it's said to be hot on some days). I managed to get my brush under a tap and shaved in a corner. Only just time to get ready – then marched in the dark to the cook-house for breakfast. I can't keep up with the pace the others eat. Then the sergeant and the corporal gave lectures in the hut. The sergeant is very much of one but probably not cruel. Then we were marched to a lecture on cleanliness, discipline and salvage, and told about leave. All there's a chance of here is a Saturday

20 The young Northern Irishman who had worked in the shop from the beginning as a packer but was now in the Army. He came back after the war and stayed for some years. He remained a life-long friend of the Hills.

evening, night and Sunday, but it must be within a radius of ten miles. After the six weeks here one is sent for two weeks to somewhere else and after that is the first leave of 48 hours.

After the lecture back to the hut, and we were shown more about how to fit belts and straps together. In the middle of that five barbers came in, and I was unluckily caught and cropped – sheared – at terrific speed. Then lunch. Then parade at once, and a lecture from the CO about discipline and cleanliness, and another about not talking. Then back to the hut, and putting on those capes. Then marched to an inoculating hut. Then outside the gates – marched to a shop to buy blanco and brass and a button stick. Then tea. Because of the inoculations we don't have to parade again till Monday. Are supposed to do a lot of blancoing and polishing and putting the straps together. I don't think it'll be easy to read. The lights are bad and there are little distractions and I don't want to. Nobody does.

Thank God it's only six weeks – though that now seems an immense time. I don't feel I shall pass any efficiency test. I seem much less efficient than everyone else. I was told that one of the tests is putting a bicycle lamp together in a given time.

We must think what we could do for my one night off which will be either the 4th, 5th or 6th weekend. We must have some alternatives in a 10-mile radius – I don't know when I shall know when. Perhaps you could find a hotel in *Let's Halt Awhile*.

The 'Platoon C-Coy' is the important part of the address. Say *exactly* how you are always.

It seems already an eternity since I left.

Love – love – love

HEYWOOD

I'm not allowed anywhere by train on that Saturday. Only by bus.

From HEYWOOD   Maidstone
                                                Saturday, 19 December
Darling Anne,

It's been just a little better today. Another man has come to the bed next to me who is quite nice. Rather strict and silent – but he understands the struggle. Every moment there's some very terrific test (of oneself, I mean). Today was mostly equipment. Thousands of immensely complicated straps and very stiff belts to get through very small stiff loops. I shall try hard not to get ill, as if one's bad it means staying longer here, and if one's not bad it means staying in the hut and scrubbing the floor. There was a great deal of blancoing to do this afternoon, and now one doesn't know what to do with all the wet things. They nearly all talk the fuck language – but it's no good trying it. I do sometimes laugh. It is so completely extraordinary. The job-allotting officer gave a lecture this morning. Said it was like a football side. If one was a good goalie one would find oneself in goal etc. (Don't repeat that.) Don't expect me to ring up. Anyhow just yet. We're allowed out on Monday evening, but at first there'll be awfully little time what with exhaustion, and all the equipment that has to be cleaned by the morning.

If there's time to send a *New Statesman* – do. I do pray you're not having a too ghastly time in the shop, and that you'll escape in time on Thursday, and that you'll have a lovely relax at Snape.

I gather it all works up into a climax of alarm here – such as climbing ropes, firing Bren guns and throwing grenades. The intelligence tests start next week.

Most of the men are 'good sorts' and no worse than indifferent – though there's one frightening one – the funny one who's always making cracks. I think of things to tell you in the night and by the morning it has all gone. How I miss you . . .

HEYWOOD

From OSBERT SITWELL   Renishaw Hall
                                                19 December 1942

My dear Anne,

Just a short line of sympathy with you . . . I could not see you on Saturday – I mean Friday – yesterday – as Violet Trefusis was there, and I'd shirked her cocktail party, as well as sending her messages about her cruelty to you and Nancy.

This letter carries with it all my best wishes for not too sad a Christmas, and a new year in which you are returned to poor Heywood . . . I can't get his present condition out of my head. It is FRIGHTFUL: but much the worst of it – as I could see from what he said – was this beastly separation from you; and you can't very well join him! . . . But surely all this nonsense MUST end SOON, though there is little enough sign of it. Meanwhile, will you some time send me H.'s number and address – I've lost it – I think you sent it me before?

If, at the shop, there are some of my sister's books and Piper's[21] put away for me, will you forward them to me here? But at your leisure, should such a thing exist.

Yours ever,
OSBERT

From HEYWOOD   Maidstone
[postmark Monday, 21 December]

Darling Anne,

I'm writing this from the 'Quiet Room'. The other half of it – screened off – is the chapel. I'm the only person in it. It was dark when I came in, but I found a light. Rather cold as there's no fire after seven, which seems rather dotty as one isn't free till about then. But there are some comfortable chairs. It hasn't been a bad day. Reveille is an hour later on Sunday, ¼ past 7. Most of the morning was spent standing in a queue to be asked about wives and allowances, and then being given a rifle and bayonet. The afternoon was entirely spent polishing brass in the hut and fixing things together. The getting up is bad enough now, but from tomorrow when we start the full days of parades, it will be frantic. One has to take down the blackout – rush for the washroom – fight for a basin – shave in cold water – fold one's blankets in a very special way – sweep the floor round one's bunk – and then be marched to the cook-house for breakfast – then come back and do one's special task (mine is cleaning fire buckets which people have filled with mud), get on one's equipment and be ready for parade – all in just over an hour.

This evening we were marched to the gymnasium where the doctor gave us a lecture on lice etc. We were examined one by one. Trousers down and balls pinched. There is a sort of light tea at four – compulsory – and then voluntary supper at seven, or you can go to the NAAFI where there are huge queues. I have generally ended by eating a doughnut. I think I'm going to get on all right with the other men in the hut. There's a publican, a bricklayer . . . They can't make me out and say things like 'What's the matter, mate, you look browned off.' They make very touching attempts to say nice things.

21 John Piper's *Brighton Aquatints*.

If it's easy to send a tiny nail brush – like the one in the shop – could you – and one of those yellow polishing cloths.

I'll write next to Snape – but suppose you may not get it. Shall try hard to ring up again one night before. Must stop as must get back to the hut for the roll call at 9.30.

HEYWOOD

From ANNE   Monday, 21 December 1942
Darling Heywood,

Am writing this in the hostel[22] while having coffee.

I feel very hopeless and ineffective today. Lots of letters and several telegrams, far too many books wanted to be able to cope with them, and I keep losing everything. Nancy is very bored with looking books up, and scarcely does it. Not very many people, thank God. Roland's[23] friend came in. I told her about our having got his picture for someone who'd seen the reproduction, and how he didn't like it when he saw it itself. Forbes[24] was there all the time wandering about without my knowing who he was, and said, 'That was me, I'm afraid.' It didn't matter at all as I laughed and said, 'How lucky I wasn't very rude about you', and he laughed, and in fact it was quite a good thing I think. We got quite friendly. It is awful how I don't know who all these people are, but I suppose I shall get to.

I haven't yet been able to move to your desk. I feel very swamped. There's about £60 in £5 or 10/- notes hidden in that place,[25] and I can't get to the bank to bank them. Nor have I got my Family Allowance Pay Book, and I should have the day you left. Nancy told someone that that Corvo picture was £12; luckily they didn't buy it. Did you tell me to write to someone about it? Don't bother to answer this as I believe it may be written in your notebook.

22 Hostel. One of a number of restaurant chains subsidised by the government where simple meals could be bought cheaply. 'British Restaurants' were the best known of these. They were run by local authorities and housed wherever they could find space. Self-service (an innovation), traditional three-course meals, meat and two veg, bangers, lots of custard – at 1/- a head.
23 Roland Pym. Painter and illustrator of children's books.
24 Alastair Forbes, a young American who fought bravely during the war, and eventually became a freelance journalist of some distinction.
25 'That place' was so secret that Anne has completely forgotten where it was. She vaguely remembers a sliding panel.

I must go back now, and send telegrams saying 'sorry all out of print' to several people. (I shan't put it so crudely really – might suggest book tokens.) Is there anything you'd like? How do you sleep, and what are the lavs, for instance, like?

A very nice letter from Osbert. I'll send it you, but send it back. I must go. Nancy'll be late for her canteen if I stay longer.

Later, in the shop

Percy Paley's[26] been looking at the Georgian Society books. Is it correct that vols. III, IV and V and the extra Irish one are £5 for the lot? He wants to know, if he had those, what the chances would be of his getting vols. I and II.

Sherston's Progress[27] has arrived you'll be glad to hear. I've sent it off.

Where is *Canadian Scenery*? Someone wants it and we can't find it.

Sunn[28] has been here hours. I've let him take away *Swann's Staircase* for 35/- – instead of £2. 2/-. He says that very shabby very old Countess of Pembroke's *Arcadia* is imperfect, and what could we let him have it for? (He is a bore.) He also got me to buy a nice book with the plans for Regent's Park, and a beastly book on Old Inns, and a book called *Three Generations of a Potter's Family*. The Inn one I suppose for someone (I hope). WHO?? The whole lot for 25/-.

(I'm going to write shop queries down as they occur, or I'll never remember.)

6.5 in the shop

Just had a Mrs Dalziel[29] row with that horrid Chelsea bookseller, Glen, is he called?[30], who stays for hours. He rooted over a lot

26 A one-eyed actor who was a friend of the Hills.
27 By Siegfried Sassoon (1886–1967). The distinguished poet and autobiographer was at one time a great friend of Anne's brother, Bob Gathorne-Hardy.
28 Sunn. A runner. See note 2.
29 Mrs Dalziel wes a good but occasionally rather difficult customer. Some time before Christmas Anne was showing her some Victorian Christmas cards when Mrs Dalziel said something that made Anne throw them all on the floor in a rage. This action she later regretted, indeed deplored. It did not accord at all with ambitions to be both a professional shopkeeper and bookseller. After the first shock, Mrs Dalziel was amused by the incident and in conversation with Heywood afterwards would refer to Anne graciously as 'my little enemy'.
30 In fact his name was Mount.

of books, several of which, I thought, might possibly be sacred reference ones, though they were probably trash you'd be delighted to get rid of. He wanted *A Book Collector's Holiday* and *Anatomy of Bibliomania* (which wasn't marked by the way), so I said he couldn't have those, but could have 10% off on the others. Then he said he gave his worst enemy in the trade 10%. So I said well what did he want to pay? Then he said what I thought were preposterously small amounts, for each, which I then began angrily to agree to. Carelessly, I agreed without noticing to the same off *The Book Collector's Holiday* (or whatever it's called). Then when he was totting it all up, I said, 'Oh no, I'm sorry, I don't want to sell that one.' I had at the beginning told him you were gone, and, in a very amiable way, that I'd promised you faithfully never to sell any reference books. He said rudely something like 'But you said you would, books are for sale, aren't they?' I then pushed the whole pile over and said 'Christ Almighty!' and he said 'Good night,' and went away slamming the door. He won't come back again anyhow. I suppose it's a dreadful thing to have a row with anyone in the trade, and they might take some fearful vengeance. Can you tell me now, what discount *should* I give to people in the trade, on new and old books?

Will you, dear, post back Osbert's letter to Snape so that I can answer it? I'll post this on my way home. Must tidy a bit now.

Fond love, darling Heywood; I long to hear more. Don't expect a letter every day from me as accidents may prevent, and the same applies to you much more, but I'll inevitably write every day even if I don't post.

The day's been all right. Fred Warner[31] came in and bought a book I can't remember the name of for the moment for £12, also a new customer – very appreciative, friend of Nancy's, youngish, called I think Lord Derwent.[32] Nancy sold him the Victorian pair of oil paintings of little girls for £10. I have an awful feeling that that's too little and they really cost £9, but haven't looked them up.

Nancy says that a friend of hers, Bridget Parsons,[33] who is now

31 Sir Frederick Warner (1918–96). A much more original and intriguing figure than his distinguished but conventional career might suggest. Joined the Navy as a boy sailor and first saw service in a destroyer off Barcelona in the Spanish Civil War. Joined the Foreign Office in 1946. Ambassador to Laos 1965–67, Japan 1972–75, and to the UN as Deputy Permanent UK Representative 1979. MEP (C) Somerset 1979–84.
32 Peter, 3rd Lord Derwent (1899–1949), diplomat and man of letters.
33 Lady Bridget Parsons (1907–72), sister of the 5th Earl of Rosse.

and for the next few months having a typing shorthand etc. course, would like to work here while I'm away. Nancy says she thinks this person would bring a lot of customers. What do you think?

Must stop, 7 now.

Love from
ANNE

From ANNE   10 Warwick Avenue
Tuesday morning, 22 December, 4 a.m. in bed
Darling Heywood,

I'm having a very annoying attack of your disease of being awake for hours in the night. I wake at 3 and don't go to sleep till 6 or 7, and then getting up is a good deal more agonising than usual. Yesterday morning I woke at 4 and never got to sleep again at all. I think I shall tell my doctor, as he always asks me how I sleep.

Your life does sound dreadful, and worse even than one had imagined. You *must* remember I think that it is an unnatural life, with normal values reversed, and not think of it all as a 'test' (as you do rather I think). It is only a test of doing absurd physical things that in normal life no one has to do, and not a test of what you're 'worth' in some way. Normal life must really be what shows the permanent values, and it is better to be Shakespeare or Ivy Compton-Burnett than the VC who shot the 150 Germans with a Bren gun. (Though unfortunately at the moment the Bren guns etc. are necessary to prevent the Ivys being shut up in concentration camps or not allowed to write, and to stop all the other horrible things that are being done in Europe and which would certainly be done here too if they could just get here quite easily with no one stopping them. I know you're not Shakespeare or a VC (and it's not really a question of Shakespeare *versus* VCs), but really it *is* better to have started the shop than just to be quick at putting straps through loops or assembling a bicycle lamp. The shop is beautiful and marvellous, and you made it; and look how people like it, the pleasure it gives, the pleasure the books give that we get for people (and pack up and send to them). It is always humiliating to do something badly that other people seem to do well quite easily; it would be humiliating if one were suddenly dumped into a team of acrobats. Imagine having the people you're with, who are so nimble with straps and lamps, coming to work in the shop; they

[28]

would be totally at sea, bewildered and useless and they could stay for a lifetime and never be booksellers. *I'm* not a proper *old* bookseller yet, of course, anything like. Don't know *nearly* enough, and don't know the stock. But I think I'm now 'fair' (average perhaps) as a new bookseller. Though I think that my great lack of natural instinctive orderliness will prevent my ever being very good at anything. Also, not being able not to procrastinate.

Hostel, having coffee, 12.30
This seems sententious by daylight, but anyhow made me go to sleep very successfully, and sleep the night through.

Calmer in the shop today, Mrs [Constance] Spry[34] came in and I succeeded in selling her that book with the unfolding plates, *Somebody's Embassy to Pope Innocent the Somethingth*, for £7. 10/-, for someone she only meant to spend £2 or £3 on. We are really getting worryingly short of stock I think, and I can't see how we'll ever get more. It doesn't look as if you're going to be able to wander about among the old bookshops of Maidstone much, and Nancy and I will be so bad at telling whether things are complete or not. Not only that, we just know *hopelessly* little really when it comes to buying old books. Only what we like the look of, and what we don't. Well I do know a *little* more that that but not much. I feel I am fairly catching up now though. I also feel there are probably at least 2 or 3 things I've entirely forgotten about. Thank God it's only one more whole day. Nothing will prevent me catching the 4 train, not if the Queen is in the shop.

Do you know it *was* Aldeburgh[35] that was bombed so badly, and Mrs Hallas was killed. Isn't it awful? The Post Office was hit too. Must go back to the shop.

5.45
Merino has taken the *Loyal Volunteers* to try to sell to someone. He said to Nancy that you usually allow him 10% on things he sells for you, but could he have a little more on this as it was so expensive. I don't know how much we paid for it – what had he better have?

34 Constance Spry, author, lecturer and pioneer in decor, in particular as regards flower arrangement, where she had enormous influence on flower decorations in the home.
35 Aldeburgh was the seaside town about five miles from Snape, Anne's mother's village.

Another thing: when I order forthcoming books from publishers – should I write to or ring them up themselves, or write to the travellers in that little booklet in your desk (if it is up to date)?

Nancy is being very good, and much better than you'd have thought. She's developing new gifts, remembering everything in the *Sunday Times*, remembering publishers miraculously, much better than me. I find myself continually asking *her* things, like I did you.

I'm terribly sorry, never got your scrubbing brush, cloth or stamps. Failed to get to bank or post office again too, but have got nearer to it, entered the things in the paying-in book. About £70 in cash – had thought of taking it home and to the bank in the morning, but daren't.

6.30

John Lehmann[36] is giving a party for Raymond's book[37] tonight, which I shall go to for half an hour. I'm rather appalled at going to a party by myself. Also, I didn't know of it before, so have horrible clothes, horrible black bag and no jewellery, and feel repulsive, long black fingernails etc.

Nancy had lunch with this new customer, Peter Derwent, who's bought more things. Lady Crewe[38] was there and Nancy said she worked near her old house. Lady C said, 'Oh yes, I've often walked past HH's bookshop, but never been inside, as I don't like going to fashionable bookshops.' Nancy said, 'Oh but we're very good, we take a great deal of *trouble* about people.'

Everybody is *extremely* sympathetic and sorry about and for you, and asks a lot and sends messages (which I forget to give you). I can't really believe that you are gone for long. I feel as if it's something temporary.

I must stop, and clear, I'm going to try desperately to remember to post this tonight.

Fondest love from

ANNE

36 Writer, critic and publisher. For many years he was editor of Penguin's *New Writing*.
37 Raymond Mortimer – *Channel Packet*.
38 The Marchioness of Crewe was Lady Margaret Primrose, a daughter of the 5th Earl of Rosebery, KG, Prime Minister.

From FRANCES PARTRIDGE   Ham Spray House
                                                          Marlborough
                                                          Wilts
                                          Monday, 21 December 1942

My dear Anne,

We were both too horrified, and very sad as well, to hear the dreadful news of Heywood's calling up. Do write and tell us about it, and what sort of a thing he has to be. He only said he was going to Maidstone, with no further details. I got his letter on Thursday and he said 'Thurs' was the fatal day, which means I suppose he has already gone off. These separations are too disgusting. I firmly believe they are the worst horrors of war. The only thing I can say in consolation is that the war seems suddenly to be going so frightfully well that I now can hardly believe it will take long enough for Heywood to take active part in it. I hope he will be near enough to get home and see you often. The news though really is terrific, isn't it? Or do you think one is madly optimistic, through having been kept so long unencouraged? After listening to the story of the new Russian offensive last night, one felt the prospect of peace arising like the Aurora Borealis in the sky. R[alph] and I both found ourselves thinking of it in practical terms – he speculating about the fate of Poland – me (I'm ashamed to say) in mere female fashion about what the domestic situation will be like in peace, and where Burgo[39] will go to school. R. has been a very good prophet, he always swore we *would* open a second front this year, and that then the Germans would go into unoccupied France.

How are you feeling, are you making a lot of Nanny-baby-plans? I hope you will secure a good old dragon – they are the best if they are funny; the fatal thing about mine was that she wasn't. May I make you a patchwork cot quilt?

I don't suppose you could face the horror of the journey down here, and the polar bear life once here, one weekend? We daren't ask anyone, but should you invite yourself some time it would be lovely. Julia and Lawrence[40] have come closer, otherwise we see no one.

39 Her son.
40 Julia Strachey. Daughter of Oliver Strachey, Lytton's youngest brother. An eccentric, witty and talented figure who wrote two good novels – *Cheerful Weather for the Wedding* and *The Man on the Pier*. Married first Stephen Tomlin, the sculptor, and second Lawrence Gowing: painter, art critic and historian of great influence and authority, and for many years head of the Slade.

Anyway, *do* write a line telling me all, for instance about what bookshop arrangements you are making.

I am wanting to order some new books, but no reviews appear. You couldn't I suppose recommend an excellent adventure classic for Burgo – like *Treasure Island* which he loved. But not too long-winded for they stick.

Both send much love and infinite sympathy.

FRANCES

From ANNE   10 Warwick Avenue
Tuesday, 22.12.42. about 11 p.m. in bed

Darling Heywood,

I only got to the party about twenty to eight (partly because my watch had got so slow), and only stayed about a quarter of an hour. I only spoke to Hester and Pru,[41] and only had one small drink; I would very much have liked two. I was avoided by Cyril Connolly. I absolutely forgot to ask Hester about Ronnie[42] which was awful. I almost feel I ought to write, or send yet another book to him.

I have been very lucky getting home at night, and have about 3 times running got a 16 almost at once (the nights I haven't I've taken a taxi; I'm giving up taking taxis again now). Tonight there was a wonderful moon.

It is very complicated remembering about the key, as I'm always last to go home, and every other day Nancy's first in the morning, so I have to drop it in her letter-box. Thank God, Nancy's first in the morning tomorrow.

I'm glad the people in the hut are amiable; that is one great comfort. I'm longing to hear what Monday was like, with all the parades and horrors.

I think the posts seem to be extremely good, in spite of what we're always saying to customers; I always seem to get your letters the day after they were written.

Ralph Redburn came in, and said you ought to pay people half a crown to do your equipment, cleaning, etc., but I expect it would be awkward. Nancy unknowingly made some unfortunate near the

41 Hester (Griffin) (see Appendix). Prudence, married to Harry Weatherall, a great friend of Hester and Julia Strachey. She sometimes worked in the shop (doing the accounts) when Anne and Heywood were on holiday.
42 Ronnie Griffin – married to Hester Griffin.

knuckle jokes about how when Prod[43] was first in the Army he rang her up and said, 'For half a crown I can get the drummer boy to' ... and then was cut off. Ralph laughed in a very uneasy forced way, and left the shop almost at once. I loyally didn't tell her what a bloomer she'd made.[44]

Mrs Sternson has given me the most beautiful dress for the baby tonight, made by her. It fortunately is really very nice, with no little embroidered bunnies or anything. What is rather a bore is that I haven't yet given them anything, and now when I do it'll look as if it's because of having had her present. I had thought of getting tickets for them all for that circus.

Wed. 12.15

Having an expensive lunch today at Carr's Tudor Restaurant (in Shepherd's Market). I thought I might just for once, as I'd got so late that going to the hostel would have meant being in a queue for about 20 minutes.

Successful morning. The piano is sold to Victor Rothschild (he'd been in yesterday and hiver-hovered). Also, you remember that pretty little book *The Orchard*, with a very pretty frontispiece. Pelham[45] had brought in the exact pair to it called *The Greenhouse* for 18/-. Nancy sold the two together for £3. 10/- to V. Rothschild (nothing very exciting but I was rather pleased, having bought *The Greenhouse*). Lady Louis [Mountbatten] was in this morning too. I liked her.

I was out when Victor Rothschild was in yesterday, but Nancy said that Mr Merino was there, and recognised him and was overwhelmed, and bowed and hovered about and bowed and hovered about, coughing, for Nancy to show him his things. VR whispered 'Who is that extraordinary man?' Nancy didn't seem to think it 'mattered', only that it was funny. In general she is getting more sensitive to things mattering, I think, and was quite cross with some friend for telling a 'coarse' story in front of Mrs Kunzer yesterday.

It is awful that you are not going to be at Snape. I shall feel very guilty as I loll in bed and think of the horrors you are undergoing.

I managed with great difficulty to get to the bank this morning.

43 Peter Rodd, her husband.
44 Ralph Redburn had been in prison not long before. Before the Criminal Justice Bill of 1966 homosexuality could be, and frequently was, punished by imprisonment.
45 Pelham, a runner.

Was nearly stopped by Mrs Fitzroy,[46] who has fallen from a bus and broken her arm *again*.

Thursday morning at home

Getting terribly late, not yet packed.

Fondest love

ANNE

From HESTER GRIFFIN

14 Percy Street

22 December 1942

Dearest Heywood,

It wasn't *a bit* the same thing going into the shop without you there; most melancholy, though everything seemed to be going with a swing, queens in uniform pouring in, Raymond [Mortimer] in a state of great complaint about something (nothing to do with the shop!), in fact the Curzon Street Christmas rush that I have so often delighted in.

But I did not really mean to call up these too familiar scenes and so make you more homesick than ever. I saw Anne at John Lehmann's party this evening, and she told me that you were finding everything very depressing except that the people in your hut were nice; I'm so glad to hear this. I am sure you will be made a great pet of by your comrades, and then just when you are beginning to find your feet, the commission question will arise. I won't attempt to be reassuring about it, it would be impertinence, but I am quite sure things will get better. I shall be so much looking forward to hearing from Anne how you get on.

On Friday Roger Senhouse[47] gave a wonderful party, in the evening, to which I went with Arthur Marshall[48] and Dadie[49] and the Weatheralls.[50] Peter de Polnay[51] may be said to have made the

46 Mrs Fitzroy, an elderly customer Anne and Heywood were fond of and who quite often fell over.
47 Roger Senhouse (1899–1970), a bibliophile, co-founder of publishers Secker and Warburg.
48 A witty and delightful man, and a professional comic writer of great success in journalism and broadcasting and, finally, on television, of fame.
49 G. W. H. Rylands (b.1902). The distinguished author, scholar and academic.
50 Weatheralls – see note 41.
51 Peter de Polnay (1906–84). Hungarian born, an extraordinarily prolific author (sixty works of fiction) who fought for the French Resistance, was imprisoned by Vichy and managed to escape back to England.

party by being dead drunk from the very beginning, and behaving like a foreigner in a novel written by someone who had had a day trip to Boulogne – waving his arms, trying to rape Prudence, then insulting her, trying to tear apart the sketch for the jacket of my book, which Roger had kindly placed on show, and finally lunging at Guy Burgess, who simply looked more offensive than ever and didn't turn a hair. Various people intervened – Dadie and Arthur staged a fight which utterly bewildered P. de P. – he couldn't make out whether it was an orgy or an imitation of himself and began to get tearful. I don't know if you have ever seen him, he is an enormous monster, like a blown-up Guardee, with a huge moustache and ungainly swinging arms and legs – and was taken away by his wife, a very refined young film extra, who was dreadfully put out by the embarrassing remarks he was making. I got nobbled by pre-Raphaelite Mr Gaunt[52] and his wife, who after ten minutes' conversation told me they were unhappily married – at least *he* did and she tried to carry it off with 'Oh William's always so *amusing* at parties' – but it was no go, he fixed her with a stubborn, miserable look, and repeated that it was the *truth*. In a way I rather longed to stay and hear more, but didn't.

Then Geoffrey Wright[53] gave a cocktail party which was rather too crowded, and again there was a considerable drink shortage, so Prudence and I didn't stay long. She is to come and spend Christmas with us, and then after that Ronnie will be going into a nursing home to have the draining operation on his leg; thank goodness he will only be away four nights and then come back here and still be able to hop to the bathroom in his plaster of Paris. Also there are going to be no dressings, which is a great relief to my mind.

I asked Anne to dine with me as soon as she was able, but she won't be free till after Christmas; I thought she was looking awfully well and not a bit tired.

This is all my news, dearest Heywood, except that I think of you a great deal, and would so much like to send you something in the New Year. I must find out from Anne what *not* to send – perhaps by then Fortnum and Mason's will not be in the *tohu-bohu* it is now – you certainly see some queer ones there about Christmas time. I was looking at a man in white flannels, a gas-mask and an ulster

52 William Gaunt had written a book about the Pre-Raphaelites.
53 A composer who lived in East Anglia and was a great friend at that time.

there this morning. Would you care for a cake, a large one, after Christmas? [In Heywood's handwriting: 'Yes'.]

Love from
HESTER

Heywood sent this letter to Anne, and added a note to it:

About *Loyal Volunteers*, it belongs to Jack Grotrian who bought it from Sawyer's for £25. Tell Merino it's on sale from a customer who bought it for £25. I think the price now could be put up to £30. (It doesn't matter if you've let Merino have it for more than 10%.)
Publishers:– Collins. Order from Mr Benson

      Allen & Unwin. Mr Shilton   all others

      Batsford. Mr Paine   from the firms

      Heinemann. Mr Hutchinson

You might get other books by Rev. E. E. Bradford. It's Routledge.

From HEYWOOD   Maidstone

Tuesday, 22 December 1942

Darling Anne,

Got back all right after ringing up last night. There's often something unexpected that turns up at the last moment to prevent – like tonight I had to go about some forms that had been filled up wrong. And tomorrow I believe there's 'Night Operations' or something.

It was *absolutely lovely* getting your letter and made me absolutely forget the surroundings, and to shout 'Yes Corporal' quite loudly when my name was suddenly shouted.

One awful effect that here has had upon me is that I can't remember any detail about what happened in the shop – like Oggy [Lynn]'s[54] picture and the Ash address (but don't stop asking questions).

Fascinating about the Ivy lunch. I'm 'rather glad you went' as Father would say. I don't expect you'll find a copy of that Aubrey book. It's v. difficult.

Not such a frightful day today. Learning about a rifle first, then marched to the gym, take everything off in a great scramble in one of those locker rooms, put on blue shorts, into the gym at the

54 *The Memoirs of Olga Lynn* were published in 1955 by Weidenfeld and Nicolson.

double, mustn't stay still for an instant (v. difficult to hear what the instructor is saying because of the echo and thumping exercises), all change places and find them again, have a pushing match with another man, run into a maze – all wildly muddling and agitating – dash out, get into uniform again, rejoin, put on gas masks and wear them for half an hour, then into a schoolroom for those crossword puzzles again, then drill, then march to lunch, then back to the gym for an 'agility test'. Eight rings on each of two sticks and two empty sticks. Each man in turn has to change the rings from the full stick to the empty one as quick as possible. I took 67 seconds (timed by a stopwatch) which was slightly longer than the average.

Then back to the schoolroom for maths test, fitting squares together (which I was hopeless at) and word test (which I wasn't bad at). Then marched to tea. Then reporting to the Orderly Room and that was all.

Tomorrow won't be much more, but the school part is mostly over – so it will mean more drilling, ending up with 'Questions from the Company Commander' which sounds frightening.

Jenson – the joke-cracker – has become the chief figure in the hut. He called the Indian Gandhi last night, and asked him how long his cock was. The Indian couldn't of course answer. I've so far avoided coming under fire from him – though he did say something about me I couldn't hear.

I get on well with the one-eyed bricklayer, who is a sort of charming ox. The publican amuses me. He has a gang of friends and they make cynical fucking jokes about everything. The talk after dark gets lewd as lewd and the noise of farts is deafening. There's always noise. Screaming wireless. The man who is next to me is quite nice but I suspect a bore. It was possible to have a hot shower bath tonight, so I did – floundering about in a footbath cubicle, slipping and dropping the soap, and naked queues waiting to get in. It's not all quite as bad as I make it sound, as one can't go on 'minding' forever, and one has moments of praising oneself about a survived obstacle. We are expected to sew, and have been told to sew up our palliasses. There's hardly time for more. It's just before lights out. The final test is taking out the blackout in the dark. I believe that on the 30th we'll be changed to another platoon, which means that an important part of the address will be different. It'll probably be all right if you write wrongly once or twice – but don't give people this one as permanent.

I'm rather dreading the dreary Christmas meal. This evening I've been talked to by a man I hadn't noticed before. Rather 'well-spoken', and has been a scout master (not queer[55] as one might suspect). I've had no twinge of sex since I've been here – only a yearning love for you – my dear, my darling, dear.

HEYWOOD

Love to Mama and Ruth.[56]

From ANNE   Thursday, 24.12.42
Darling Heywood,

Am now in a 1st class carriage in Liverpool St. (Ma[57] is paying the difference). It's *Bedlam*, and I've been in serious anxiety that I really wouldn't be able to get on – different porters kept leaving me at different wrong platforms. I have been missing you very much I can tell you.

We have finally decided not to open the shop on Monday. A guard has just locked us first class passengers in (only 3 of us) and angry 3rd classers keep trying the door and cursing us; I feel guilty. Now we are off.

I feel *very* tired today I must say, hardly able to move. A headache in the morning, but I stopped it with a lot of aspirins before lunch. The baby seems quite all right anyhow, and kicks more and more, once in the night so hard that it woke me up.

Mrs Sternson gave me a present of a little wooden box with a poker-work old-fashioned lady on it this morning, holding spills. *Fortunately* it's *meant* for the shop, where in fact the spills will be very useful. I've said about the circus, and I think it was quite well received; luckily he doesn't get an afternoon off till Tues. week so there's plenty of time. If poss. I'll get the very best seats. I gave Mr Lester[58] a pound, Smith £2. 10/- (he has really been good, working as late as 9 o'clock some nights) and Jimmy [Smith] 30/- (he hasn't been at all bad either; this morning I arrived rather late, and he'd actually tidied the books on the tables very nicely, and was dusting the ones on the shelves).

You can't imagine the mass of old trash (horrid *new* old Nature

55 'Queer' was the accepted slang word for homosexual, as 'gay' is now.
56 Ruth Gathorne-Hardy (see Appendix).
57 Anne's mother Dorothy Cranbrook (see Appendix).
58 The man who cleaned and firewatched at the shop.

books etc.) we've sold. I made a great effort a couple of days ago, when the tables were almost bare, and got out lots of things from the Red Room (F), and high up on BW,[59] and they've practically all gone, and there are *no* worrying little piles one feels will never be got rid of. You wouldn't like the Raymond Mortimer book I suppose, would you? It's very good indeed I think.

Mrs Dalziel came in yesterday afternoon, and we were tremendously nice to one another; she said how we always had such *lovely* things in our shop, and where were you? And when I told her, she was very upset and sorry, for you and for me, and said she was almost a pacifist really. And she thought you looked so delicate, and what a worry and responsibility it must be for me. Extraordinary, really rather wonderful of her, and a great relief. She bought a French book for £2. 10/-.

Snape, Christmas morning in bed

Some very nice presents. I love yours my dear, very nice to get it – very pretty indeed. Also got a large cameo (Grecian profile and harp kind, nice) from Ma, and a small one from John (Hill)[60] (whom I haven't sent anything to).

And various scarves and stockings from various people, and rubber sheet and apron. Handsome cheques from your Pa and Ma, and a very very handsome one from Fidelity. Also a scarf from Mother and a pair of man's gloves from Father (obviously out of his own store, good brown ones; I'll give them to you).[61]

Now your letter's arrived; lovely to get it as I haven't had one for a long time, and thought I might never here, country posts being bad. You *couldn't* have known that Cold Ash address as it was a customer of mine, a Mrs Rowntree. The strange thing is that Lawrence Gowing, who was in the room when I was telephoning the telegram, said it was Rosamond Lehmann's address.

Oggie Lynn got her picture all right; it and she came the same day.

What a menace the joke-cracker sounds.

I miss you here very much. As devoted though I am I get slightly

59 The walls of the front room of the shop were red; F and BW were abbreviations for the names of shelves. F meant 'front', BW 'big white'. Necessary for cataloguing.
60 See Appendix.
61 See Appendix for Fidelity (Cranbrook) and Heywood's father and mother (that is Pa and Ma *and* Father, and sometimes Daddy and Mummy; Anne's mother was almost invariably Mama).

irritated by Ruth, Antony and Mama in combination, and it used to be so splendid going away for walks, and getting into our room at night.

Ruth has just come in to say about Darlan[62] – what a wonderful thing to happen, solving everything it seems (or solving a lot of things anyhow). I wonder what will happen.

The war does seem to be going wonderfully well. Charles [Lambe] says cutting the Veronezeh-Rostov railway is tremendously important and good.

Have got to get up and go to church now. Forgot about church and didn't bring a hat, so will have to go in a scarf.

Fondest devoted love to my darling Heywood from

ANNE

From HEYWOOD   Maidstone
                                              25 December 1942
Darling,

You seem to have been doing wonderfully and heroically at the shop. *Please* don't worry over it too much. I think that the not sleeping is due to having to think about so many things. I found your letter – the serious part – very encouraging and very true. I'd been trying to say something like that to myself – but rather falteringly – and it makes it much better what you say.

What the hell of a bore it is being a 'shrinker'. Thank heaven we found each other.

Wednesday was a violently hectic day, and it ended with 'night operations', which meant scrambling about in a wood and mud in the dark, so I didn't get out till late. Stood in a queue for three quarters of an hour to ring you up, and was the next person to go in, when it became too late and I had to go back.

Before I forget – about money – I can't think why Tom[63] told me to bring so much. I spend almost nothing. So I'm sending back the £2, and don't send any more. Save it up for the weekend or house

62 A French admiral who was for a while Commander-in-Chief of the Vichy forces. He eventually came over to the Allies, despite strong anti-British feelings, a move which led to his assassination for suspicions that he was still pro-Nazi by a fanatical Gaullist – Bonnier de la Chapelle.

63 Tom Harrisson. Author and co-founder of Mass Observation. A friend of the Hills, he started in the Army earlier than Heywood and had written to him describing his experiences and giving him advice.

expenses or anything you like. I'm incapable of bribing anyone or giving drinks to the NCOs. (Jenson does that.) One has to talk about cunts the whole time. I've offered some of the nice ones supper and things but none will take it – it almost offends them. I went with two to the YMCA last night in Maidstone – the bricklayer who is sweetly stupid and another little man who is nice – tho' it's a struggle to say the right thing. I'm beginning not to like so much the man I did like.

Firing a Bren gun was fairly shattering and there was a swearing officer who paralysed everyone. Next time we have to fire 75 rounds from it. It's the hand grenades I'm dreading most – but that won't be until the 4th week.

I must answer some of the shop questions. Just had the Xmas dinner which was good. Goose and plum pudding and beer. A *terrific* shindy of shouting and singing and bawling. I've escaped to the icy church hut. They are most of them playing cards in the next hut.

Answers to questions. Are you sure you haven't got the Family Allowance pay book? I remember you saying something about something like that which had come the day I left. I've heard men say that their wives haven't got their pay yet – it takes some time to get through.

The Corvo picture is £30 (or £25). I wrote to that man in Essex about it and told him to write to the shop. The man who bought the other, I can't remember his name. His address is Tendring Old Hall, Tendring, Essex. (Later) I've just remembered, Holmden is his name.

I go to sleep fairly soon at nights but still wake early, in spite of getting up at 6, chiefly because of a man next to me who starts a shrill internal rumble at about 4 o'clock.

The lavs are not bad. One can lock oneself in alone. I get very constipated in spite of the exercise and thousands of Taxols.

Georgian Society Books vols. I and II are v. difficult to get. I've cliqued them several times. A whole complete set is worth quite £20. They were published during the last war and so are scarce. I believe really that those vols. we've got ought to sell for more than £5 altogether, as I bought that extra vol. separately. I think we ought to get £7. 10/-. But if Percy Paley says he would have them for £5 it wouldn't matter.

If Mr Pain from Batsford ever comes in, you could ask him that sort of thing, He's very helpful. *Canadian Scenery* ought to be in C.5 (or one of the lowest of the top shelves of A.B.C.D.). It's got cellophane round it. Or did Merino take it on approval to try to sell it? I remember he was threatening to.

That *Arcadia* is one of Harry [Clifton]'s books. I should shuffle off Sunn by telling him it belongs to a customer who wants a high price. I should think about £5 would be the value. You might be able to trace one in *Book Auction Records*.

I don't think I ever wanted *Three Generations of a Potter's Family*. Am sure I've never heard of it (unless it's *The Wood Family of Burslem?*).

It's splendid you've got rid of Mount. I always wanted to be rude to him even when he never spoke. 10% is an absolutely all right trade discount on all books. A great many booksellers such as Quaritch never give any more. I only did when I thought the book was unsaleable otherwise. If you're undecided you could always say you must write to ask me. I'm sure that Mount isn't in the least in with the rest of the trade.

I think perhaps it would be a good idea for Bridget Parsons to come.

I shouldn't rush into buying things you're not quite sure about – even though the stock is low. Something really nice does turn up if one waits. And I may be able to do more when I get out of here. Also there will be sales starting again. If you sent me catalogues, with a stamped envelope to send them back in, I would look through them. Will you tell Hester when you see her that I loved getting her letter and enjoyed it v. much, and tell her too that I may be some time answering as I don't have time to write more than at the most one a day.

If people suggest sending things, it is really only tiny little bits of food that are the best. There's nowhere to put anything, as no personal thing is allowed to be visible, even inside one's locker. Cigarettes are welcome, because one has to stand so long in the queue at the NAAFI.

I may send you a parcel of disgusting washing one day.

You really do seem to have sold a wonderful lot of things.

As one only sees Maidstone in the dark, it's a job to find the hotels, but I'm going to try and find one where we could stay – if I get that night. I might not because of my helplessness with the NCOs. We could anyhow have dinner.

Love my darling,
HEYWOOD

I'd quite like the *Times Literary Supplement* – only when you've finished with it.

From ANNE   Snape
                                    26 December, 11.20 p.m. in bed
Darling Heywood,

Have written all the thank you letters I can think of this morning; my hand feels quite stiff.

It would be wonderful to have supper at Maidstone next week. I was thinking, if you have to be back by say 9.30 I might as well go home that night; if you can stay till 10 or 11 I'd stay the night. I realise that at the last moment you mightn't be allowed to come, and will expect that. Though I shall be very cross.

About leaves, try not to have any between the 7th and 14th of Jan, or the 4th and 11th of Feb (copy this in your diary). They are days when the Curse would have been due, when one is more liable to have a miscarriage Mr Saunders[64] says. After 2 March I fear all dates are prohibited according to him. I shall anyhow be a mountain I suppose.

I'm having a wonderful rest here, sleeping extremely well and feel quite different. How do you sleep in your hut? Would you like some Sedormid?

One relief is that I did find the shop less bad than I expected (before you went). I had felt it might be more than I could stand, and that it could just be impossible, but I don't feel that now. And though there'll be terrible arrears to catch up on when I get back, and also probably dreadful letters arriving, I'm not worrying at the moment at all, not nearly as much as before you went.

I think it might be a good thing if you wrote to Nancy saying I'd said she'd been so splendid etc. As indeed she has. The thing about the shop is, it has now got such a momentum of its own that so long as there are reasonably sensible people there to manipulate the machinery, it carries itself along to a certain extent. I think it may increasingly bear the imprint of Nancy's personality and not ours/yours but I don't think that really matters. Better than if it merely became more and more negative, which I think would have happened if I'd had just some dim person to help me, however efficient. When you get back, it will all get back and be the same as before,

64 Anne's gynaecologist.

and better with any luck. The great thing is, in the war the competition from other shops is so much less. For instance, people kept on coming in straight from Hatchards, complaining of them like anything. Evidently they quite lost their heads in the end, and said that everything they hadn't got was out of print (and then when people came to us they found it wasn't true, so that was rather good). The real difficulty with us is going to be re-stocking.

I must stop, and get up, and go to the post.

Fondest love from

ANNE

PS Nancy's article you see in this *Lilliput*.

Will you say what we are to give Merino for the *Loyal Volunteer*? I've remembered now it belongs to Jack Grotrian and I have an awful feeling he wants a fearful lot for it. Merino sold it for £25, and wants if poss. more than 10%.

From ANNE   Snape

Sunday 27 December in bed

Darling Heywood,

Everything is the same as always here. Antony and Mama[65] in good moods on the whole. I'm afraid I don't think my scheme of getting Ma to London so that Antony and Ruth can be alone together here is going to work.

Jonny and Sammy notice your absence very much, and miss you, saying things like 'Where is Heywood? Why isn't Heywood here? I do wish Heywood was here.' Antony and they are very good together now; but as usual he gave them terrifying presents, appallingly sharp assegais this time.

The day before yesterday Mama was shouting from her bed to Mary and Nettie,[66] Jonny and Sammy, in turn. Jonny came running and she shouted, 'You needn't come upstairs, just bring me my matches and cigarettes.' Jonny said, 'Is that all? You were making such a noise I thought you must be dying and wanted me to take your false teeth out first.'

I find myself longing for you very much in a sad and melancholy way in the long evenings here.

65 See Appendix.
66 Anne's mother's two Scottish maids. Mary was Mary Buchanan. Nettie eventually married the gardener's son and became Nettie Brown.

Nothing much more to say I don't think.

Fondest love
ANNE

From HEYWOOD   Maidstone
Sunday, 27 December

Darling Anne,

I can't get a room for you on Thursday. It's New Year's Eve and everywhere is full. We could have dinner however. You could come by a train which leaves Victoria at 5.18, and catch one back which arrives at 10.15. And do hire a Relyonus taxi to meet you at Victoria. (*Do* do that.) If you stayed the night we should only have about ½ an hour more together. Friday is no good as we are inoculated that night, and the weekend is uncertain also because of that. It's all a bit risky because one never knows what ghastly thing will turn up. I asked the sergeant if he thought I'd get away by 6.30 on Thursday, and he said he'd fix it (but he might not be about that day). If I am not on the platform go to the hotel – it's called the Royal Star – about 10 minutes' walk from the station. I've booked a table for dinner at 7. Start if I don't turn up and if I'm not there by 8.15, ask for an ABC and take the train back. If it's foggy, or if the whole thing is *at all* too much of a business, or if you're tired or ill, don't come. I'll try to ring up in Tues. or Wed. night and we'll talk about it.

Thanks so much for sending the little box of things, I liked seeing the little box again. I enjoyed the toffees v. much. It's v. nice to have something to put in one's pocket for the immensely long mornings. If you come, bring a few cigarettes if you can (I feel like some awful Lady Power the way I ask you to do far too many things).

This week has not been so exhausting at the end, because of the rest on Christmas Day. I felt very low indeed that day – but yesterday was better. I'll tell you about yesterday. After breakfast – sweeping floor, cleaning buckets, cleaning rifle. Parade at 8.30. March to parade ground which is about ½ a mile away. You have to carry the rifle in an awkward position, so it feels as if one's hand's coming off. On to a football field where we had to do firing exercises – throwing ourselves on the ground and loading and firing dummy cartridges. You carry shorts and gym shoes with you, for next you go to the gym. After the rifle business we went to the gym, where this time we had to leave our boots on, but take everything else off. Put on shorts and only a pullover. Then marched out of the camp and made to run a long way down the road. Some fell out. Then back again to the gym, change again, on to the parade ground and drilled by the sergeant. The CO suddenly appeared and inspected us. I was passed by. He told one man to shave, and said that our brass wasn't nearly bright enough. Then marched back to the hut and given a lecture on gas. Then marched back to the parade ground again and more rifle drill. Then marched back again for lunch. After lunch blancoing the equipment which took till 4. After that – being Sunday – we were free. I went out with the Indian and went to the cinema, *Queen Victoria*. After that went to the hotel and had a good dinner, which was wonderful. I was at sea as to what the Indian would think about the place, but he seemed very pleased and to enjoy it. He's nice and hates the whole thing here. He's 42. Talks in a shrill voice. He's been in England for 20 years, is an export merchant in Ilford. Has got a wife. I wonder if she's Indian or English (she may be coming on Thursday night so we might see – I don't think any danger of them expecting to join us). The hotel is quite large, and is the sort of place where they wear paper hats, so be prepared for that sort of horror.

It'll be awful for you coming back to all the aftermath at the shop. I got a letter from Viva [King]. She seemed pleased with the present. Wanted to know who it was by. (I could tell you a way to find out.) A tiny bottle of fountain pen ink is another thing I could do with if you come down – not important.

I waited for the Indian while he telephoned, and heard him referring to me as 'my boyfriend'.

The bricklayer is very touching. He came up to me yesterday and said he'd been thinking during the night what he'd ask to be, and that he thought he'd ask to join the 'Pigeon Corps' – because he was very fond of animals. He didn't know if there was a Pigeon Corps. There's another little man I'm quite friends with called Eric – more middle class. Has only been married 6 months and is pining very much. He had a car once and likes dance tunes. Then there's a carpenter whose home is near Worthing, and he knows Aldeburgh. He is a short fat little man. The other morning he was made to fall out on the parade ground and show how badly he had marched – with his head down and not swinging his arms.

The publican is the centre of a group of beer drinkers. Very cockney and tremendous swearers and farters. (There's a slightly repulsive one next to me – oldish and bald who makes immense noises and whose feet steam.) They are kind to me if in difficulties with a strap or anything. The man on the other side – Shackitt – says prim things about the others to me. 'Disgusting.' He makes tiresome general remarks to the whole room. There are also some rowdy youths.

All love
HEYWOOD

From ANNE   Started at Snape, finished at Warwick Avenue
29th December
Darling Heywood,

Starting straight away about the shop, as I've just been spending hours going through my notebook and letters and the clique reports. Now I've just been looking at your 'What is it' notebook, and it is full of things uncrossed out that you didn't tell me about (or that you may have told me about but if so I've quite forgotten). Do you think they are still valid or not? Far too many for me to copy out and send you. Do you think I'd better post the whole book to you? Ghastly though it would be for you, or if it got lost. The thing is I'm so tormented now in the shop by people coming in and asking about things they've ordered that I know nothing about, and also runners coming in with answers to *Clique* adverts I know nothing about or whom they're for etc. For instance, Xmas Eve just as I was going, a man brought in a huge book about garden ornaments in answer to an advert, and I can't find anything about it in any notebook or letter.

Next morning
All right, I've just found the letter.

I think *probably* everything not crossed out in your notebook is valid – do you think that would be so? For instance *Trelawny of the Wells* to John Bigham, Turgenev's *Sportsman's Sketches* to Roger Kidd? There are hundreds more. I feel overwhelmed by all the books people want, and wish they'd stop ordering anything for a month, and cancel everything they have ordered.

Have the books by Sir Harold Boulton for Lady Boulton been

[47]

cliqued yet? I can't find out, as I fear I've lost the last *Clique* (it may turn up).

Questions crowd to my pen as I go through the beastly *Clique* reports. Perhaps Nancy may know the answers to some of them.

                                                    In the train, 7.50
Having the most intolerable journey. The train keeps stopping for ages and ages. Now we're about a few miles from Liverpool Street; we have been stationary for over three quarters of an hour. However, I have got a seat (middle) which I was very lucky to get as there were already hundreds of people in the corridor even at Saxmundham.

                                    Home, about 10 to 9 (having supper)
Lovely long consoling letter from you. Don't bother or be harassed by all my *Clique* fusses etc. at the beginning of this letter.

Maddening interruption has just taken place. The lodgers knocked and came in (they obviously think I must be lonely and need cheering up) to play a new record of theirs on the gramophone; they were being kind and were nice, but I wanted to go on writing to you.

How dreadful wasting all that time to telephone and then having to leave.

It's all right about the Family Allowance Book – I'd forgotten I'd sent it back to the Paymaster General at Edinburgh, and it was at the Post Office. I'm getting paid. I'll keep your £3 for the weekend, and not send you any till you ask.

Percy Paley has bought and paid for the Penguin Society thing. Yes, Merino has got *Canadian Scenery*.

Hester [Griffin] has rung up and I'm going to have dinner with her tomorrow. I wish I'd said I couldn't rather, as it's such an effort. I'd rather stay at home and write letters to you than go out, by far. But one does like seeing her.

                                    Tuesday, 29th, at lunch in hostel
Another lovely long letter in the shop this morning, which I have instantaneously lost which is very tiresome. Especially as it's full of vital things. However, I think I catch a 5 something to Maidstone on Thursday, and if you're not on the platform go to the Royal Something hotel and wait for you there. If what you said is totally

different perhaps you'd better send me a wire,[67] though really I think I'm *sure* to find the letter eventually.

It made me laugh what you said about the bricklayer wanting to join the Pigeon Corps. I told Nancy and she said there really is one, and Lord Tredegar is very important in it. He has 'Pigeons' written somewhere on him.

I'm *completely* swamped under at the shop, and don't see how I can ever emerge again. There are about 30 new books wanted and every post brings more and more important orders. Also there's been a misfortune about Eddie Sackville-West *again*, which I can hardly bear, a book he wanted sent to someone, sent to a totally utterly wrong address. *My* fault somehow too. And the accounts (day book etc.) weeks behind-hand. And I've lost a clip of special bills urgently to be paid. I'm not sparing you my miseries you see.

Fondest love. How dreadful everything is. The Bren guns sound a nightmare. Anyhow, wonderful to see you Thurs. I shall be prepared for a miserable disappointment, and not to see you at all, up to the last minute. I do hope I find your letter.

The weekend did come off.

From NANCY MITFORD   31 December 1942. Shop
My dear Heywood,

Many thanks for your letter – Christmas wasn't too frantic and very profitable I hope. You would be amazed at the havoc wrought in the shelves – almost a bore as there is hardly anything to show people or make traps with! Merino hung about like a well-meaning warlock, and we sold 2 little horrors for £7 each for him on one day, and a £5 one the next, so I think he was pleased and so were we.

I think Anne seems very well and now all is much slacker, and Mrs Frieze-Green (well named I consider when you think where she's going to sit)[68] will provide I suppose further alleviation, so I wouldn't worry.

67 A 'wire' was a telegram – at that period, and for many years, a reasonably cheap and extremely useful means of sending urgent messages. Now replaced by very expensive and much less swift Telemessages. Telegrams can now only be sent abroad.
68 See Appendix.

Anne's glamorous brother[69] has just asked me out to lunch so I must tee up a bit.

Love from
NANCY

69 Eddie Gathorne-Hardy. See Appendix.

2

Maidstone, 1943

From FRANCES PARTRIDGE   Ham Spray
2 January 1943

My dear Anne,

Alas – I am afraid Heywood will have gone off and it will be very sad and desolate for you. I do hope he will eventually be fitted into some literary and harmless position suitable to his intellectual gifts. But even that I fear will not make up for separation in the least.

This is to ask you if by any chance you could put R and me up for the night of 1 Jan, a Tuesday? It would be lovely if you could, but say if in the slightest degree inconvenient, and we can doss down elsewhere and would hope to see you some other time of day.

Perhaps you could come with us to a movie that evening, if not otherwise occupied, or unless there is nothing you want to see.

We have seen nothing for over a year, and would enjoy anything.

Christmas has left us more dead than alive but 'went off' as they say pretty well. We had a grand party with a conjuror and Christmas tree – rather an effort, but the conjuror was very good and produced wonderfully pretty things, from tambourines and hats.

R. is having a great struggle against being called up for Home Guard.

Yesterday we made our New Year prophecies with the help of Julia and Lawrence and I am now suffering from the reaction.

Much love
FRANCES

From HEYWOOD   Maidstone
Tuesday, 5 January

Darling,

I've been trying to write, but it's been particularly desperate.

Yesterday I was told I must have my hair cut again, which meant standing 2½ hours in an outdoor queue. Then another hour in a queue for supper, and making the bed in the dark. This afternoon we were marched to a field and had to crawl and roll through mud with packs on our backs, rifles and tin helmets – literally roll with the rifle between our legs for over two hours. Then at a quarter to six I was detailed for fire fatigue, which means you can't go out in case of fire, and at the same time for taking down all the Xmas decorations in the mess hut. Mercifully that task was put off at the last moment. It would have meant climbing about among rafters.

We've got a new very strict sergeant who last night after lights out, when all were asleep, came in, woke everyone up, and made some change their beds round because we weren't all sleeping alternately head and feet. It gets faster and furiouser each day. I long for Saturday and seeing you again. I may not get there till dinner. The chemist fell unconscious today. I *might* get there for tea. I might be altogether kept in for some frightful reason. Could you bring a few old rags for cleaning. I don't expect apples are possible. Not at all important. Lights out.

Love, love
HEYWOOD

Wednesday, 6 January
I never even managed to get this scrawl posted today. The new sergeant is devilish. There was vaccination tonight. More queuing in pouring rain. Tomorrow I've got to be tested on the parts of the Bren gun, which I'm in a great fuss about. Also there's an inspection by the CO, so everyone has been cleaning up the whole evening. I've been fumbling and fiddling and getting into a great muddled mess with blanco and brasso, and it all looks far worse than before. The grenade throwing is on Friday, so that will be over by the time I see you. I had to ring up early on the chance tonight – it was the only time. Your letter[70] arrived when I got back, which was very nice. What ghastly times we are both having – both so miserably cornered and so much fret. You must always go home and read a novel at 6. It doesn't matter if the shop founders – though I know it's bound to be all appalling for you.

70 This letter has not survived.

I was fascinated by your account of Mollie's[71] and Nancy's iciness. Is she very smart? Of course you won't get this till Friday now, and you'll be able to tell me. Awful that this is my only communication this week. I *must* go on polishing. All the others are and I am far behind. So deadly boring, and cold and filthy. I hate being got down by it all but we all are.

Love my darling dear
HEYWOOD

I say – how terrific about the Partridges coming. I'm very jealous.

From ANNE   Wednesday, 6 January. In shop
Darling Heywood,

I wrote to you once today but have lost it. One question if possible to be answered by return. How much shall we charge for those two railway prints that have been couched[72] for ages (one of a tunnel, one of various old engines)? Someone of Nancy's urgently wants to know.

I won't go on writing as I'm staying late on purpose to write up the day book while no one's here.

Have got to go to Norway all by myself tonight – am very frightened. Nancy says she (Norway) is going mad. All's been well today, though rather hell at times (all right now).

See you Sat. Probably won't write again.

Fondest love
ANNE

PS E. Joseph[73] clamours to be paid. Did we keep St Simon and something else (I forget what) on appro from them?

Later

The week's middles do seem extremely long I must say.

What a ghastly life. It really is. Effort effort effort, and separation. And yet one must still consider oneself lucky, obviously, unquestionably; but though one knows that, it's hard to feel it.

---

71 Mollie Frieze-Green.
72 To couch. A shop term invented by Nancy (origin forgottten) meaning to add to a pile of books or objects on the floor or elsewhere. These were set aside for some purpose – to be priced or called for by someone or sent back from a sale, any of many reasons, some of which were sometimes forgotten. The pile was called a couch.
73 Well-known antiquarian bookseller in the Charing Cross Road.

From OSBERT SITWELL   Renishaw
                                                         11 Jan
My dear Heywood,

Your letter reached me just as I was becoming desperate about where you were, and what might be happening to you. I don't think that it's made me feel any better about what *is* happening to you, but anyhow I can communicate and condole . . . It wouldn't matter of course if life was long: at least not so much, but to have to go through all this in order to have one's life shortened is too much. And one can't cultivate Nostalgie de la Boue to the degree to enjoy it.

I find the snow and frost *here* as much as I can cope with. Today it is simply one long slick down Russian Mountains, and the cold in the house I believe must be *worse* than anything *you* could imagine. But at any rate there's food and drink: so that when I think of your terrible days, nausea attacks me – but *of course* the shop will be all right; Anne will see to that. Because she's very clever, and lots of endurance.

Malcom[74] has been bombarding me with 1880 photographs and I can think of no reply – David[75] has just been here, and sent you his love. Otherwise I've seen no one, and have no news, which doesn't make correspondence easy.

I was given 5 lovely huge volumes (1770) of a French book on the Realm [?] of Naples; do you know it? I can hardly move for books – and bills.

I hope to be in London before long, and to hear that you are on leave. Your health can't stand it. It's madness of them putting this sort of work on you, when you could do something more valuable so well.

                                                      Yr. affec
                                                      OSBERT

74 Sir Malcolm Bullock (1890–1966). An army captain in the First World War and later an MP. A diplomat and Francophile. Commandeur Légion d'Honneur – 1954. A great friend of the Hills.
75 David Horner, the young man who lived with Osbert Sitwell.

From HEYWOOD   Maidstone
                                              Wednesday, 13 January
Darling Anne,

This[76] came today (open again!) and I've rushed through it and put tentative prices which Nancy could leave with Mr Osborne if she thinks they are nice enough. If condition is bad, don't bid. There's nothing frightfully thrilling that I can see.

Not such a bad day today. I went to ask for the weekend, but he said I'd have to ask the new company commander, and so I shan't know till Thursday or Friday, and it'll be unlikely as they say he's strict.

The weekend was a lovely break. It's awfully poignant seeing you in those tiny snatches.

Could you send me £1.

                                                        Love
                                                          H

From ANNE   10 Warwick Avenue
                                      Wednesday, 15 January, after lunch
Darling H,

I have a roaring cold today. Luckily was anyhow going to work at home today. (This morning actually didn't work at all, but slept.) If I'm not better tomorrow I won't go to the shop I think, so as to be all right for the weekend *in case* I can come to Maidstone.

I miss you and want you more and more at home I find. I long inexpressibly for you to be sitting on the sofa reading now this minute. I find myself having fantasies of your getting minor injuries or illnesses, and being discharged from the Army, and go through all the details of the process of your getting home and arriving, and then *being* at home again.

I must stop and pay bills. Simpkins[77] have 'stopped supplies'.

Don't get too got down. The time *will* come when we will have an ordinary life again, blanco-less and agreeable.

                                                        ANNE

76 A Hodgson catalogue of a forthcoming sale that Heywood was to mark with suggestions of what to bid for, and how much. Hodgsons were book auctioneers in Chancery Lane.
77 Simpkin Marshall supplied books to the trade from the publishers, but at a smaller discount. W. H. Smith succeeded them.

Heywood was allowed home leave for the following weekend, but had to be back on Sunday night, the 17th. He and Anne dined in Soho on Sunday evening. A raid started which turned out to be the worst there'd been for some months, so he saw her home, which caused him to miss the last train back to Maidstone. He left Warwick Avenue early on Monday intending to catch the first morning train.

From HEYWOOD   Maidstone
                                                    Monday, 18 January
Darling,

First obstacle was the bridge over to the underground (at Paddington), jammed with troops. Took ages. Got to Victoria at 6. Told the 6.10 to Maidstone was off. No train till 7.18. Went to Grosvenor Hotel. No breakfast served till 7.15. But found buffet open. Went to sleep in train, woke up to hear 'all change'. Bomb on the line. Had to go by bus. Didn't get here till 10. Met another very stupid man who'd done the same thing as me; he was more hindrance than help. Reported to guard room. Called out and taken to CO. I told him what had happened, and about your 'condition', but he said it was no excuse. That he'd been in London and had left his wife and children to come back. He put me 'on a charge'. I don't quite know what that means – but I have to appear somewhere tomorrow, I don't know where, to be given a verdict. Probably it will be a week's confined to barracks, and doing extra duties like cleaning out the cookhouse. A great bore is I shan't be able to ring up, and next weekend will probably be quite impossible. Otherwise I'm not particularly got down by it – it melts into the general bloodiness. The weekend was lovely and made me feel much more sane. You are so wonderful my dear – I can't tell you how but you are and I do adore you. Blanco – Brasso – Blanco. I've just done the belt with the wrong one. Two people – the Indian and another – had done all my marking, which was wonderful. So extraordinarily nice of them. I do wish I had time to write longer letters.

                                                              Love
                                                               H

Could you send my £2 and some stamps. If Mrs Sternson made a cake I would like it, but don't particularly bother.

Darling Heywood,

Have been indoors all day, except to the pillar-box to post a letter to you and Mrs Kentall. (I rang up and asked for you to be sent the £s and stamps by Smith, registered; hope they arrive.)

Had a great fright the morning after the raid, as Mollie never turned up. I really thought she *must* be bombed, as I decided it was inconceivable she would be like the Smiths, and just not turn up because she was tired, without telling me. There seemed no other alternative. Really she was having her hair done, and had told me she was going to on Saturday, but I had forgotten.

The Indian has just this instant rung up with your message – he *is* nice. He sounded exactly like a woman on the telephone. I couldn't think of enough things to say or questions to ask him – could only rather *over* thank him.

My cold is extremely bad, my ears humming with quinine. I paid a lot of bills during the day, and got extremely bored by them. I will do the same tomorrow.

I feel pangs of pity and pain for the poor shop, all alone with Nancy and Mollie and going to be left so much more alone for so much longer when I have the baby. I do hope it will be all right. Really this is silly perhaps, as they *are both* very good, and in fact each of them their own way is better than I am, Nancy with her greater confidence, and knowing so many more people than I do, *as well* about books, and Mollie being much better and quicker than me at doing the accounts.

But for both of them it is just a wartime job they happen to be doing, and when the war is over they will do other things, or if the shop went bust tomorrow they'd just do a war job now instead of a shop one. Their futures after the war would be no different either way, so they have no worries. Whereas for us the shop is our livelihood and our life and we know how precarious it is, how easily it *could* founder, which they have no idea of at all. It would be *so awful* if you had to go back to working in someone else's shop again, being ordered about, for the rest of your life.

Anyhow things do seem to be going quite well at the moment, And when the war is over with any luck it will be like it was before with us, *our* shop, and it could be much better still if it prospers and becomes less worrying than it's been so far. So we must hope.

I suppose you *are* CB,[78] as the Indian was allowed out and not you; I wonder what it all means and wish I'd thought of asking him what the verdict was and what was happening to you. He said you were 'all right' but probably only out of kindness to me.

I wish I had the strength to tidy the shop but I find that in my present condition I literally cannot carry and lift even a few light books about the place for more than 5 minutes or so, so the awful piles and heaps remain and moulder, and more form themselves. I do wish Nancy would deal with them. I suggest it sometimes and she says 'yes' but never does and never will.

Palewski,[79] who thinks everything we've got is expensive, thinks the Doré *Sainte Bible* is 'pas cher'.

When I rang Gladys up I was told she was in the public Oxford Square shelter, all covered with black spots, infecting everybody.

Ralph[80] came into the shop yesterday. It was very nice indeed seeing him and we were able to talk quite a bit. He was *extremely* sympathetic about you.

Mr Sternson says there were over 200 casualties in that raid, 90-something of them from our shells. There are rumours from many sources that there was a very big bomb that killed about 20 people in St John's Wood, which is mysterious as surely we should have heard it, but perhaps it was before we got back.

A call-up thing for you to fire-watch has come saying if you don't comply you'll be fined £500 and sent to prison for 2 years. I expect I shall forget to answer it, and that is what will happen to you.

I have taken 2 more quinines, and now I am quite deafened by my ears buzzing. I feel quite alarmed and wonder whether I have taken too much, and if perhaps it is very bad for the baby. But surely it would say on the bottle if a perfectly ordinary common medicine is death to the unborn. Or Mr Saunders should put it in his list of things not to do, like driving 100 miles or 'riding horse-back'.

---

78 Confined to barracks.
79 Gaston Palewski, of Polish extraction, was a distinguished French politician (particularly associated with de Gaulle) and diplomat, who had a short affair with Nancy Mitford. She continued to see him and remained in love with him for the rest of her life.
80 Ralph Jarvis, a cousin of Anne and an old Cambridge friend of Heywood.

Thursday, 21 (still at Warwick Avenue not yet shop)
Just after lunch. My cold is worse than ever today. I haven't had
such a bad one for ages. No complications but just complete
stuffed-upness, ears too. I've given up taking quinine or anything
but am just enduring it. I try to take an extra lot of liquid. I began
to wonder whether it might be the beginning of chicken pox, but
Gladys says it doesn't begin with a cold.

Merino is beginning to be very tiresome now. He is definitely
putting up the prices of the things we have on sale or return from
him without telling us. Twice *after* we'd sold something (those
paper-backed French books) he said we owed him more than we'd
charged the customer. I've at last got him to do a list, and I am
meaning to find everything and compare. Two things I have already
looked at; the set of Doré (which is now 14 instead of 16 vols as he's
sold 2), he has written in his list as £25 to him, and it is marked
in your handwriting £20 quite clearly. And the set of Boccaccio's
Decameron I had marked £8, he now says is £9. I shall have to go
through it all, and then tackle him about it. Also I have slight
suspicions that sometimes he makes me pay for things we've paid
for already, but this is probably not so. I also think it is possible he
genuinely forgets what he has said before. But it is a great bore. My
heart sinks rather now every time he comes in.

Later about 3
That wretched little beast Jimmy has been given your letter to give
me, but isn't bothering to bring it.[81] I have just taken my temperature; it's rising slightly, only 99.8, but I think I'll go to bed. Don't
feel the slightest anxiety though, as I know exactly what it is, a
'feverish cold', and if I stay in bed and keep warm it will get all
right.

If you are Confined to Barracks one consolation is that I couldn't
have come to Maidstone anyhow. I should be in misery if you were
able to get out and I couldn't go. I long to hear what sort of a time
you are having.

Dearest love from
ANNE

81 Jimmy Smith lived only a few doors away.

From HEYWOOD   Maidstone
                              Tuesday 19 January [posted 20th]
Darling,

I was marched to my trial this morning. Marched in to the room
where the CO was. Told to get out as I'd marched in badly.
Marched in again. Given 7 days CB. That means never going out,
and reporting to the guard room several times a day, and being
given extra duties. All very boring, but still it's only a week. The
first time I have to report in ¼ of an hour after reveille – I can't
think how.

I forgot to buy a table knife. Could you post me one – fairly soon
as it's tiresome not having one.

I'm finishing in the dark. I was made to do things till 10 last
night. Send food if you can.

From ANNE   10 Warwick Avenue
                          Thursday, 21 January, in bed, about 5.30
Darling Heywood,

I was appalled to get your scrawl about the ghastly CB thing. It
seems too cruel that you should be made to do any extra when you
were already doing so much too much, and I feel guilty as I fear I
didn't try hard enough to stop you seeing me home on Sunday
night. I am hoping, though, that the week began on Monday, and
that therefore there will perhaps be only 3 more days, of which
perhaps Sunday won't be so bad.

Beastly Jimmy only brought your letter about half past four. I
rang up the shop and told Smith to post a knife to you. (I hadn't
the face to ask Mrs Sternson to, though then you'd have got a
better knife, as she too has got a terrible cold and ought to be in
bed like me.) My temperature went up to 100 for a bit (but is
going down again) and I am very deaf in one ear. The awful thing
is that Nancy had arranged to go to her mother from Saturday
till Wednesday, and now she has had to put it off. I urged her
nevertheless to go, and to let Mollie be alone in the shop if necessary. (I don't *think* Mollie'd mind; it might be quite fun for her.)
But thank goodness Nancy is insisting on not going. I expect to be
able to go to the shop again next Wednesday; I shall be very annoyed if I can't, and I think I might be quite all right by Tues.
Luckily before I left I had done nearly all the things like writing to

Harry[82] about the steamboat and to the press-cutting agency about his racehorse, and during the last few days I have been able to pay all the angriest bills, and quite a proportion of the patient ones, so I don't feel so worried as I might do. In fact it is rather nice really not being at the shop. If only you were here though, or at least were not in such a dreadful situation.

Don't, if you can possibly help it, get driven too mad by it all. They obviously think that 'this will teach you what the Army is'; and I think the impression you should try and create (remembering that this is a special test place) is of 'realising it's all in the game,' and of not minding or caring or even thinking about it's being unfair. The trouble is, it must be physically and altogether much too much. I can't bear to think that it is now about 7, and you may have another three hours of horrible labours, while I lie here comfortably in bed. But anyhow only another week of *this.*

I wonder if I'll be able to see you on your way through?[83]

Tomorrow I will try to ring up Fortnum's and Harrods to see if they have any nice suggestions of not-on-points food to send you.[84] Did you get Wesson's[85] chocolate all right? I'll send you some more of that tomorrow. Though it's not very good I fear. I suspect that in America special shops advertise that they'll despatch things to England, and that they really swindle all the Wessons and charge for expensive chocolate and only send muck.

Morning, 22 January

I think I will give this to Mrs Sternson now, to post when she goes shopping, so that it will get to you nice and early. I'm about the same this morning, perhaps a bit better if anything, but I've hardly

---

82 These, whatever they were (Anne has no recollection), were typical of the bizarre tasks Harry Clifton set the shop.

83 Heywood was to be posted on Wednesday, 27th: it was not yet known where to.

84 There was no 'points' system for food. Presumably a mistake for unrationed, though for tinned foods and sweets each person had so many points to use on what they liked. Food was rationed by coupons, so many for each item. At first only bacon and ham (4 ozs a week), sugar (12 ozs) and butter (4 ozs, later 2 ozs). From January 1940 gradually everything was rationed, until only fish, offal, sausages, vegetables, and eggs were left. These were rationed by long queues.

85 Wesson Bull, an American friend who had been best man at Heywood and Anne's wedding.

ever had quite such a frightful nauseating nose etc., and do feel quite ill (though not *gravely*). I'll go on staying in bed.

Fondest love

ANNE

From HEYWOOD   Maidstone

[postmark Thursday, 21 January]

Darling Anne,

I'm going to have hardly any time to do anything now. I hardly have time for meals, Will you tell the Orchards and everyone I shan't be able to write. I have to do menial tasks between 6 and 8 a.m. Yesterday cleaning the lavatories, washing out filthy dishes in the cookhouse and swabbing the floor. Also from 9-10. Last night carrying benches to the sergeants' mess, and filling a bus with great hampers. That goes on till Tues. morning. Tues. night we're confined anyhow as it's the last night. You'll remember to send the money, won't you? I've no stamps either. The other men go on being very nice and help me with my cleaning. Have to get up ½ an hour before reveille as have to report at guard room at ¼ to 7. Tell Malcolm [Bullock] I can't write.

Love

H

From HEYWOOD   Maidstone

Thursday, 21 January

Darling Anne,

Lovely letter from you. It made me feel better. It's fairly desperate now with these extra punishments. One is treated like a criminal. But the great thing is that it's only 4 days more, and all the other people are so nice. The Indian is marvellous and does a lot of my equipment for me. How dreadful about your cold. *Please, please* take care and neglect everything to take rest. I can only write rather incoherently just now. It's quite impossible for me to get out again before I go. Do write as often as possible to say how you are, even if it's just two lines.

Now, 6 o'clock, I've got to go off to the guard room and be given some ghastly task for two hours. One man in the room got the same sentence for having his straps crossed wrong.

Let me know where you'll be all Wednesday, just in case I can ring up or go through London.

All love

H

Darling Heywood,

Having a terrible spate of bad luck lately with Malcolm [Bullock]. He ordered *Story of San Michele* about 3 weeks ago. The publishers said OP [out of print], which I told him, and I've been cliquing it without success. Today he rings up Nancy and says it *is* in print, and he's got 12 copies from somewhere else on his desk. Then, about a week ago, he rang up ordering £5 worth of thrillers. I suggested getting review copies from Ralph Partridge, so as to get more thrillers for the money, which he thought a very good idea, and I wrote to Ralph. Today Malcolm rang up in a rage saying why hadn't they come, they'd been promised for the 21st. Well, he'd not said one *word* even about being in any hurry at all for them, let alone giving a date. He said could we get them today. Of course Nancy said no. So he stumped off to Hatchards for some other thrillers to send instead. I would have got them from there for him myself, if I'd been in the shop, and I wish to God I had been. I *think* we're probably eventually going to lose his and the Red Cross's custom, by a sort of inevitable process. He exaggerates every failure, and minimises every success. And this nightmare of Stationery Office Books failures will clinch it.[86]

I'm better today, and have an awful feeling I'm going to be quite all right by Monday, which will be very awkward as either I go to the shop, which will be very annoying for Nancy as it will mean she needn't have put off her mother, or if I don't, it will be annoying for Mrs Sternson having to cook another lunch for me, and I shall seem a malingerer, and feel one.

Did you get the £ notes all right that Smith sent? Mrs Sternson has sent you a fruit cake today (a bought one, probably not very good, but something to eat anyhow), also more of Wesson's chocolate. I

86 Malcolm Bullock had, among many other things, the task of collecting books for the Red Cross. It should perhaps be emphasised that this series of outbursts was completely unlike him and must be put down to the considerable stresses and anxieties of the war at this time.

tried ringing up Harrods and Fortnum's, but absolutely everything needed points or coupons; also they couldn't promise to send before several days. When I'm up again I'll go out with the points and see what I can find.

Sheila[87] has lent me Dr Gibbon's *The Care of Young Babies* which I'm plodding away at.

Saturday, 23rd

You have been wonderful about writing, throughout all the difficulties. It has made a great difference to me knowing. I wonder if you get all the letters I write to you? Your letter I got today seems to have been written on Thursday and you seem only to have got one letter from me. I posted my first letter on Tuesday, and have posted one every day since then. My first letter was partly about how nice it had been your having an extra half night (not then knowing the ghastly results of this). Did you get that? [No he didn't.]

Today I am glad Nancy *is* going to be in the shop next week, and doubt if I shall be up to it; I feel very 'pulled down', and my nose is still nauseating. I have to use face-towels as handkerchiefs; it is all very squalid. I am better though.

Quaritch is advertising for Doré's *Sainte Bible* this week. We are boldly quoting it at £10 – I expect they'll be horrified.[88]

It's wonderful Mollie being in the shop when I'm ill. It means when I get back there won't be the ghastly arrears there normally are – pages of Smith's and Jimmy's books[89] to copy out and add up, and pages of day book to enter. She's doing all that.

I will give this to Mrs Sternson to post now. I *expect* I'll be in the shop all Wednesday. Will let you know for certain on Monday. I shan't go out that night anyhow in case you telephone.

Later

Have been up (in my dressing-gown) for lunch and tea. Felt low, depressed, stuffed-up and head-achy and have gone to bed again now. Mrs Sternson is being very kind. I miss and want you badly (did you get my letter saying how much I miss you?) and it is awful to think of you struggling alone in a sort of dreadful desert far away

87 Sheila Hill (see Appendix).
88 Price today between £200 and £300 depending on the binding.
89 They kept the 'stamp book' showing the cost of posting books and letters.

for goodness knows how long. But don't minimise the misery to spare my feelings, will you, and neither will I my lesser miseries.

Later, after dinner
Nancy came in for about half an hour on her way to Norway before dinner. Was very nice, and made me laugh a lot. She urges me to go on staying at home until I feel quite all right, and so I think I shall, as they seem to be getting on very well really (apart from Malcolm) without me; and, after all, will eventually have to. When I feel a bit better I can go on paying bills here.

Sheila's book about bringing up babies simply appals me, it seems so difficult. I've given it to Mrs Sternson to read.

Harry [Clifton] rang up this morning (passed on to me by Nancy) and ordered the speedboat! I hope it's still available. He said rather sadly that the British Museum never had written to him about his MS – do you think it would be possible for me to write to Aunty Wormald jogging him? I hardly know him. I'm getting on very well with Harry just now – he is sorry for me about you having gone – I made him sorry for you too – he was quite interested. He didn't ask for money which was rather wonderful, as I'd sent him a bill showing a £230 credit.

Sunday morning, 24th
I don't really feel any better – nose and ear blockages as severe as ever, temp still nearly 99. If I'm not better tomorrow, I'll ring up Mr Saunders I think; he might be able to give me something. I dare say pregnancy makes one's resistance lower and makes one take longer to recover from things like colds.

Hope your Sunday is being slightly better that your other days.

I shan't be able to send you the *New Statesman* this week, I'm afraid, as I'm now in a dreadful period when the news stores have stopped letting me have it, and it doesn't yet come from the *New Statesman* itself (it's supposed to from the 13th). I've got Nancy's sacred one now, which I must return this evening. There was none at Paddington. Nancy tried.

I must stop, and will get Marlene[90] to take this. I do wonder if I'll see you Wed, and where on earth you'll go to.

Fondest love
ANNE

90 The Steinsons' daughter, then aged eleven.

From HEYWOOD   Maidstone
                        Friday, 22 January [posted 23rd]
Darling,

If you're still bad do make Mama come to fuss around you. It'd
be awfully good for her too – and distracting for you? Do, please.

Today has not been so bad. Yesterday was hell. An exhausting
day of parades including bayonet practice – stabbing sacks and
jumping over and into trenches – a sort of lunatic frenzy. There's a
notice board in the middle of the field saying 'Remember Hong
Kong. Suppose a yellow man raped your mother, sister, wife . . . '
We got filthy which meant an enormous cleaning. Then getting
back I had to report to the guard room with the other 'defaul-
ters'. Made to double backwards and forwards up the path. Then
sent to the kitchen of the sergeants' mess and given huge filthy
dishes to scour out. A confusion of steam and grease and bawling
men and boiling water, and of course I couldn't get the grease off.
Then unchoking blocked-up sinks and scrubbing tables and the
floor. That went on for 3 hours till 9 o'clock. The Indian saves my
life. Buys buns for me and cleans my rifle and equipment. He's
Christlike. Today I've got off the 6 o'clock reporting and fatigues
because of a merciful inoculation. Also a less violent day – though
more bayonet.

I think I left my gloves behind. Would you keep them until my new
place. I'm sure to lose the extra pair I luckily had. The money has
arrived but I haven't had time to get it yet – one has to go to a special
place for registered things and there hasn't been time. Only 4 more
days. We all say that every hour. I'm very anxious about you.

                        Love – darling Anne
                                        HEYWOOD

From HEYWOOD   Maidstone
                        Saturday, 23 January [posted 24th]
Darling,

Thanks so much for the wire and your letter. I do wish I could
ring you up to find out how you really are. Any asthma? A sort of
dawn of dotty hope is reaching over me. Chiefly I think because of
the sort of general feeling here of end-of-term. . . I should think it's
quite probable that if there's a gap before the next job they'll keep
me on here for a bit. But I don't know when they'll say. Possibly not

till Wednesday itself. Could you bring yourself to ring up Hester about my cigarette case (it's wooden) and keep it for me? It was useful because now the cigs fall out in my pocket. What endless pestering little jobs the shop and I make you do. I know that sad feeling for the shop.

The Indian thinks he may go to the Intelligence. He had to fill in a form about it. His wife has got 'flu too.

Today has not been so bad. By mistake I got up at ¼ to 5 instead of 6. Blundered out to the wash-house – it was nice having it to myself, and I took a long time shaving and washing my hair. Lights went on at ¼ to 6. Had to report to the guard room at ¼ to 7. Was sent to the cookhouse to bring back a pail of tea – it slopped a great deal on the way, but it was too dark for the corporal to notice. Why is it that with us things always slop? Breakfast ¼ to 7. Feverish preparations for drill. Parade at 5 to 8. Supposed to be an extra special smart one. It went without disaster. The chemist – who was behind me – said to the sergeant, 'May I fall out, sergeant? I'm a bag of nerves.' He was not of course allowed to. After that a little lecture on Ack-Ack. Then feverish change into battle order – tin hats and all – and marched out for more bayonet practice. Then another lecture on Ack-Ack. Then to the gym – change into shorts and boots and made to run along the road and do exercises on a grass patch in front of a bus-stop. Made to lie on our backs in the wet and touch the ground behind with our heads. One bewildered old woman waiting at the bus-stop. Then report to the guard room again. I got off without fatigues. 10 minutes for lunch, Then all the kit to be laid on the bed for inspection by the company commander. The sergeant screaming fantastic instructions. I think he's rather mad. I often want to laugh. He's one of those real army sandy-haired sergeants who bleed easily and who have been in India and are full of barrack-room ditties. Tremendously stupid. We were all in a fever by the time the volcanic commander came in, but he was in better than usual mood. I had not stamped my hair and clothes brush with my number and was told, 'You must be bloody daft, man', which is comparatively amiable.

I do hope my next job will have at least some faint purpose, in that I'll be some good at it. It's mad to be so pointlessly wracking oneself.

I must try to join the little group by the fire now and not seem too aloof.

I think it's very unlikely if I go on Wednesday that I'll be able to see you. An NCO goes with us. My conviction ends on Monday night. I think they'll keep us in on Tues, but if I get a chance to ring I will.

Love
HEYWOOD

From HEYWOOD   Maidstone
Sunday, 24 January

Darling Anne,

Have just rung you up. A bit of luck that was. The chocolate is *wonderful* to have. V. splendid of you to send two slabs.

The nickname for this confined-to-barracks which I'm on is 'Jankers'. There are a great many jokes about the 'Janker boys'. Four from the room are on it. One for a wrongly crossed strap, another for a dirty rifle, another for a rusty spoon, so my crime is comparatively enormous. I think Father Orchard[91] is in a great stew and thinks my 'career' is ruined. When anyone asks me where I'm going the right answer is 'Fucking jankers, mate' – but it doesn't come out correct.

I was on church parade this morning and sang 'Onward Christian Soldiers'.

Very probably I shall not be able to write tomorrow or Tues. I think the phoning unlikely as they confine people in case they might know their unit, and tell people.

It was lovely to hear your voice – and not so ill-sounding.

H

From ANNE   10 Warwick Avenue
Sunday, 6.30 p.m., 24 January

Darling Heywood,

It was a wonderful surprise – hearing you on the telephone. What a *relief* that tomorrow is your last day of torture.

Dr Mac[92] came this afternoon. He said I had very severe catarrh

---

91 See Appendix.
92 Anne's brother Antony's wartime partner, who was later killed. Since the custom in private practice then was that any surviving partner had to 'buy out' the partner who died, this cost Antony a great deal of money.

(a bad cold which I knew). But he has given me a prescription for some inhaling and spraying stuff, which *was* worth his coming for, as really my nose is *hell*, and gets not the slightest bit better. Today I am using those triangular bandages with pictures of bandaged limbs, fingers and heads as hankies, tomorrow I think there is one more triangular bandage in the Red X box, the next day I'll tear up a night-dress, the next day, *I hope*, the wash'll come. He says I mustn't get up till my temp. is down, which really is a relief, as it is no pleasure. But it all makes me rather ashamed, as I'm sure Mrs S never went to bed for a cold during her pregnancies, but went on with her work perpetually to the last minute. And would have even if her temp. had been much higher than mine is.

I wanted to speak to Dr Mac about you, but he was in a great hurry, going to tea with Lady Carnarvon.

Another rather shaming thing is that I am not knitting and sewing for the baby, as I lie here in bed idle. Mrs S commented. I wouldn't mind, for half an hour or so, if I knew how, either.

Monday morning, 25th

Two wonderful long letters from you today. How *ghastly* cleaning all the bloody dishes and floors, and the lavatories.

Yes, I forgot to say Father rang up last week and was *appalled* when I told him about your fucking jankers – and very irritating. He said, 'Oh, Heywood *shouldn't* have done that – you can't do that sort of thing in the *Army* you know.' And when I protested rather shrilly, he sort of soothed me down while obviously going on thinking the same. They think you've been 'naughty'.

I've just written to Ralph [Partridge], telling him what a hurry Malcolm's in about the thrillers – I also quoted bits from your letters, to be read and lamented over breakfast at Ham Spray.

I *fear* I'll still be here Wed. if you can ring me. I am fretting rather over the poor shop I must say, being away from it for so long.

I shan't go on any more, but will give this to Mrs Sternson to post this morning, so that it is sure to get you. Angel noble Mrs S has washed some of my unspeakable handkerchiefs; too wonderful after days of triangular bandages and towels.

I do *long* to know what'll happen to you next, and if you'll be near.

Fondest dearest love from

ANNE

Monday [probably 25 January 1943]

My dear Anne,

I had a letter from Heywood today, so reply at once – he told me his address would be changed and you would forward it – I have written him *such* a boring letter; but what can one say, except sing the Miserere. I have no news, have not seen anyone.

I received a bill today – and will pay it *as soon* as my legacy arrives. Incidentally, I had, as you surmise, only one copy of *Not Me, Sir*.

I hope you are getting on well, but it must be sad and distressing for you. The whole thing is too *rotten*, and that's all there is to be said about it.

It's filthy here, and I'm concentrating on some new symptoms; I become hypochondriac (can't spell today), when depressed, do you?

I hope to be up soon, and come to help you and Nancy.

Yours ever-affectionately

OSBERT

From ANNE   10 Warwick Avenue
Monday, 25 January (not finished till Saturday 30th)

Darling Heywood,

Mollie came this evening, with a mass of bills, cheques, letters, and receipts, ledgers and queries. Your bed has become like an enormous desk, covered with little piles. Rather a good thing I think, and will stir me up a bit. I feel better tonight; Dr Mac's sprays and things are rather a comfort, and my temp., though up this morning, is right down tonight, which is the best way round. If it is down tomorrow morning, I will do shop work in bed in the morning, have lunch in bed and sleep all the afternoon, and get up for tea and dinner. These luxurious little plans must be rather em-bittering for you to read about, when your cold is probably quite as bad as mine is. I shall be here if you *can* ring up on Wed. Of course you won't get this, now I come to think of it, till long after you *have* rung up if you're able to.

Tuesday about ¼ to 8 p.m.

Have been doing exactly as planned; am now downstairs, Feeling better than last time I got up. The speedboat arrived at the shop this morning, and Harry [Clifton] came and took it away. It cost us £35 and we've charged Harry £40; wish I'd charged more rather. He was *very* pleased with it apparently, as well he might be, as it sounds a wonderful one, and goes 30 miles an hour, so the shop we got it from says. Also, by writing an imploring and very personal letter to the Stationery Office I've got them to send the full 50 *Coastal Command* that the Red Cross want, and 25 of the 50 *Front Line*, which have gone today, so I feel better again about the shop, in spite of a number of rather harassing delayed and undealt with letters brought by Mollie last night. Mr Goldberg keeps writing and ordering Upton Sinclairs. One rather awful thing is all Red Cross bills now have to go monthly to Malcolm, instead of to kind lenient harassed Miss Henderson. I'd rather like *him* to be conscripted into the Army and sent to Maidstone too along with Jimmy.

Now you've just rung up. I feel a little bit depressed, I must say, at your going all the way to Salisbury Plain to this beastly RA Regt.

Now Mrs Sternson's just been in and has cheered me up a good deal by saying that Mr S often goes to Salisbury Plain for the day for races, and that it only takes 2 ½ hours – better than Snape.

On Wednesday 27 January Heywood was posted to an artillery regiment at Larkhill on Salisbury Plain. He had one hour at Waterloo on the way through, where Anne met him and they had a quick sandwich lunch. Then he joined up with a number of other soldiers who were going to the same place, all carrying their rifles and kit bags, many accompanied by their wives and children, or 'sweethearts'. Anne walked with him. Before they reached the platform someone they knew slightly rushed up saying 'Hello! How are you? I think the last time I saw you was at the Arundel Ball.' She walked with them to the platform and went on 'chatting' in a style they found increasingly embarrassing as well as maddening until the train went off.

[Continuation of Anne's letter]

Thursday, 28 January

My dear what do you think, Aunt Janie's died, the night of the day before yesterday. I must confess it was a great shock to me, and the

[71]

tears welled up to my eyes.[93] I had had a letter from her dated Tuesday, extremely sympathetic, and indignant at your CB, and saying she was going to make all my baby clothes. She also said she'd been in bed with a cough, which she'd been rather enjoying, but 'my enjoyment is wearing thinner which means I am better but still rather tired of too much cough and too little sleep. However, I fell I shall be well again soon.' She died that night in her sleep.

Another outstanding piece of news is, I've had a letter from Mrs Kentall[94] saying she'd like very much to come to the shop! But she is really supposed to work in a factory; however hoped to get some sort of medical way out of that. It is not definite until she knows about that, but she *wants* to.

The Waterloo hour did not do me any harm, though as my temp. isn't *right* down I've decided not to go to the shop till Monday. Nancy's not going for her holiday till I'm quite all right and is being very nice, not in the least making me feel guilty.

I felt extremely low and depressed all yesterday, and I cried a good deal.[95] I think this thing must have been a kind of 'flu. One must remember, when one feels very depressed, that *inevitably* before long feelings of hope and optimism will return. I long to hear about your new place – I wonder if you will be able to ring up ever? Father rang up last night from Aunt Dorothy's.[96] He said she's got a cake going stale waiting for your address.

Friday

Now you have just rung up. (I'm constantly being very let down by the telephone just now, as the Sternsons have a friend at a distance who keeps ringing up and I think it is you.) It sounds rather peculiar this specialist squad – a bore about the trigonometry I must say. But when you said 'unsuitable' I feared something to do with tanks and big guns and this would not be as bad as that. Biddy[97] came to lunch yesterday, and I was encouraged by her

93 Anne's aunt, Lady Jane Gathorne-Hardy, an intelligent and witty woman who had been crippled by polio from the age of four. After her mother's death in 1931 she had bought a house in Vence, where she remained until 1940, when she returned to England in a coal boat from Marseilles. Somerset Maugham was among the passengers.
94 See Appendix.
95 There was much talk at this time of a second front, which made Anne frightened for Heywood.
96 Heywood's father's elder sister, wife of Sir Robert Knox.
97 Biddy Harrisson (see Appendix).

saying that she went on railway journeys up to the last minute with both her babies, so I hope I shall be able to get down quite a lot if you can get off.

There are quite a lot of little pieces of news since yesterday. Both Antony [Gathorne-Hardy] and John [Hill] came to tea today which was rather extraordinary. John said that Sheila had got jaundice and had been in bed for a week (he'd been down there for the night).

Antony said that Eddie was in Cairo, staying with Patrick Kinross[98] on his way to Baghdad. Isn't he lucky? Charles [Lambe] is back, very brown and fat and his wrinkles all gone Peta says. *When*, I wonder, shall *we* start having a nice time again, instead of leading lives of bleak endurance as we are now? Endurance and apprehension, what a waste of life, that one could be so enjoying. But how *much* worse many other people's lives are. One has to remind oneself continually of that. But that being so doesn't really cheer one up, it's just another extra distressing fact to think about.

I went into the garden today, which is looking wonderful; everything sprouting, some of the bulbs about 8 inches high. What were those things that you planted round the edge of the border near the door in the front garden; and that you cut back for the winter? They are *very* alive and well-looking. The carnations you planted are looking curiously alive too; they were never cut back and they look just the same as after the flowers were first cut off them; but I don't think they can really last all winter.

A slightly better-toned letter from Malcolm which I enclose. I am not sending people your address until your letter comes tomorrow, as I feel I might have got it a bit wrong on the telephone.

98 Lord Kinross, formerly Patrick Balfour. He had been married to Angela Culme-Seymour but now they were parted. His house was three doors down from Anne and Heywood in Warwick Avenue.

3
Larkhill, Salisbury Plain

From HEYWOOD 14335674 Gnr G. H. Hill
(You must call me A Battery, Specialists Squad
a Gnr, though I am 4th Training Regt., RA
a specialist Gunner) Larkhill
Wilts
[Postmark Friday, 29 January]

Darling,

We got here about 8. Long wait in Salisbury then shunted off to Amesbury. Confusion in dark of sorting kit-bags. Then an awful scramble into a high lorry and a 4- or 5-mile drive. All put in a v. crowded hut. Marched to blanket store – supper and bed. It's like starting again. It's now after breakfast. I hope we'll be reassorted today, as am almost entirely with youths of 20. I am going to ask for all sorts of boring difficult little things. I'm sure you have a famine of *rags*, by now, with your cold. There might be a pair of large white pants in my drawer which I could tear up.

Clean *vest*. Then there's a sort of fizzy stuff for cleaning spoons and getting rust off things. Mrs Sternson might know its name. But that might be impossible.

Do hope you are not worse for Waterloo. It was wonderful being able to see you. I should have sunk into utter gloom if it hadn't been for that. I think you oughtn't to start going suddenly back to the shop for all of every day.

Later

We've been sorted. I was put into a little group of 6. All the others into drivers and gunners. We were called 'specialists'. We were interviewed, one by one, by two officers. The first thing they asked me was was I good at maths. I said no which worried them. They said I'd been recommended as a clerk, but no clerks were really wanted by them. That I had anyhow better try the course for a month and see what happened. It means logarithms and trigonometry so I can't think what will happen; but anyhow it's a great relief to know I'm not going to begin to be a gunner. This course will be mostly classes I think – with a little drilling, and PT about 3 times a week – so it should be less strenuous than Maidstone, though Reveille is ¼ of an hour earlier – at 6, and the lessons go on till 5.15.

It's a windy high bleak place – quite near Stonehenge. 12 miles from Salisbury. Amesbury – which is the nearest town – is about 4 or 5 miles away. There are buses. The other specialists look the sort of brainy grammar school sort. It's very funny really, don't you think, that I am a specialist.

I'm going to try to ring you up, but am told there are immense queues at the telephones. They've emptied the hut a bit now. There's a special 'specialist' one I'll go to, but it won't have any room till Monday.

The full course of this thing lasts three months. I think it's awfully doubtful if I get the 48 hours that weekend. They tell me one isn't allowed to London, which is maddening. We might perhaps Partridge?[99] Find out from Saunders if it's still all right for you to travel about.

A bit of soap too I'd like (not too large). If you send the things all at once, perhaps better register – it doesn't matter though.

Love
HEYWOOD

[Continuation of Anne's letter begun on 25 January]
10 Warwick Avenue
Got your letter now. I must say I'm rather pleased you're a specialist. From your letter (but perhaps you're being very brave?) it doesn't all sound too bad.

I keep trying to ring Hester about your cigarette box, but the telephone always seems to be wrong – perhaps Ronnie's iller and the receiver's off. I'll write. I will send all the keys I can find, with the vests and hankies and rags, and perhaps some will do for the

99 That is, stay with the Partridges. Ham Spray was about twenty-eight miles away, near Hungerford.

little box. I will send this this morning as perhaps it will then get sorted etc. sooner and arrive sooner.

Fondest love
ANNE

10 Warwick Avenue
Saturday, 30 January, 5.30 p.m.

Darling Heywood,

Am feeling much better today, though still stuffed up. ('More myself'.) Have done a great deal of bill-paying which is a relief. If *only* we can now get Mrs Kentall. What's worrying is that there's a brand new thing about only being allowed to engage women under 45 through the Labour Exchange. I thought I might go to the Labour Exchange sometime and find out and plead – they might be able to put her immediately on it and off it in some way.

I hope you got my parcel all right. I *think* there is everything you wanted in it, but no food I fear. Do you want more rags still? As there are any amount of old shirts and things in a trunk in the spare room (ones that used to be in the shop and that you put to be thrown away), I think bits of some of them might do for clothes for the baby, but there are any number of other bits for rags.

Ought we to get *Book Prices Current* – latest vol. advertised in the *Clique* 32/-? Also *Book Auction Records*?

Where is our collection of newspapers? Someone's advertising in the *Clique* for them. How much shall I report them at?

I am very sad to have missed that glass picture at Maidstone. I now remember it as being the most beautiful glass picture I've ever seen.

Morogh[100] came in this morning and said that Churchill had been killed; he has been told this by several people, but not on good authority. I do wonder. I rang up Nancy but she had heard nothing. She's going to a French [Free French] lunch, and is going to ring me up if she finds out anything. She *promised* to bring the *New Statesman* on her way, but it is now 25 past and she hasn't been. I am wanting it *terribly* to read at lunch, and now this moment.[101]

100 Morogh Bernard, who then lived next door to Anne and Heywood at 8 Warwick Avenue, with his wife Didi and daughter Maria.
101 Owing to the paper shortage only small editions of magazines and newspapers could be published. The *New Statesman* – quite apart from the fact they enjoyed it – was important to the shop from the point of view of ordering books that had been well reviewed.

I must say I slightly shrink from plunging back into shop life again, after the sheltered secluded lazy comfortable time I've been having here for such ages. I expect I shall make terrible discoveries.

Evening 8.30 Sunday

It evidently isn't true about Churchill.

Peta [Lambe] rang up, and said Charles has had a very narrow escape. There were 2 aeroplanes for his lot of people to go back in, and he had to decide which one to get into. He looked at their numbers, which were 43 and 44, and decided 44, and got into that one, and the other one crashed and everyone was killed, including his opposite number in the Army.

During the last few days I've paid about £600's worth of bills, all but Smith £100, Faber £80, and a few other little ones amounting to about £60. We've still got about £270 in the bank at the moment. The rent and electricity and all those sorts of things are paid. (Strangely both the electricity and gas are a good deal less than last year.) So I think that's not too bad, if sales *now* go on all right. I'm going to make a great effort and add up the day book the next weekend I'm at home, and see how it all compares.

Will post this early tomorrow, so that it gets you Tuesday all right.

Fondest love from

ANNE

IMPORTANT Where is your little camera? I would like to take it to Salisbury if I go next weekend.

From HEYWOOD   Larkhill

Sunday, 31 January

Darling,

I've just spent two hours sewing 6 little bits of coloured flannel on to my sleeves. They are called flashes – those inexplicable things one sees on soldiers' arms. I kept sewing the sleeves together. The result is crooked. There was meant to be a church parade this morning (there's a warning just going) but it's such a howling raging blizzard that it's been put off. We got fairly soaked getting to the parade ground.

It was typical at Vivian's.[102] An old Greek queen, and a very

102 Vivian Macan, a wealthy solicitor friend.

young officer, and a worldly refugee lady who had called. Vivian bustling round and lighting candles and making it cosy-cornerish, and a lot of silly chatter about bogus Greek princesses. I felt rather resentful – I think because I had expected a lot of sympathy and to be asked questions. I had tea and a glass of sherry. On the telephone Vivian asked me to stay to dinner, but when I said I must go at ¼ to 7 he didn't press at all – I think he was thinking there would not be enough food for the lady who had lent him £200. However I had a lukewarm bath, and any private house seems wonderful, and Vivian was just like he really always is. I'm rather appalled by how awfully sorry for myself I feel all the time – without much cause. When you think of the people in Libya etc.

I went to a hotel, had some dinner, and caught a bus back, which didn't mean immense queues as I'd thought.

I shan't be able to ring up much. After sixish there's always delays on the line. The first time I tried for two hours. And the telephone box is on the main road with all the glass broken, so very cold.

These are impressions of some of the other specialists: 1. Old Charterhouse man. Faded-handsome, vain, humourless, uninteresting. Calls me 'Hill, old man'. He's the only one who was also at Maidstone, and the one I should be friends with, but we don't contact much.

Two young – just from Cambridge – men. One very bouncy. I should think very clever. Has said he plays soccer, acts, reads poetry, has a girl friend in Chiswick. The other one I don't know about yet. They are great friends. The rather frightening mysterious younger generation. Interesting.

An elderly depressed man – who doesn't think he'll be able to do the course because he's only been to a council school. Looks like a sex-starved parson.

A bright red-faced Welsh boy.

A clerky ex-surveyor.

A competent upright rugger player.

What I would like would be some nice sly shy subversive person.

Have you been able to send a handkerchief yet? Mine are beginning to have a horrid smell. I managed to wash one at Vivian's. My cold is better today. I think it's a good deal that which has been making me feel so low. I don't think about the time every moment here – like I did at Maidstone – how long it is going to be. The youths in the room make a lot of noise and fight and crash into the bed, but don't seem to take personal notice in remarks. There's a wireless continually, but not too loud, and sometimes it gets me and I feel like Ruth, and when it plays 'My Only Sunlight'[103] I think of you and cry.

There's a peculiar man on the top of my bunk. Spectacles and hair going grey, and hideous like a Hinks[104] – mutters, never talks to anyone, and no one speaks to him. I have asked him a few civil questions, but he has only mumbled. I have noticed that he has a Penguin George Moore's *Confessions*. I have lain out my *War and Peace* as obviously as possible to see if it will melt him.

I think it will be OK for you to come to Amesbury next weekend There is a hotel there. If you are *sure* the journey won't be too much. Quite likely a long joggy bus. Evidently everyone does go in without a pass. I am going this afternoon to meet Derek[105] without one. Am frightened though after last awful thing. They told us here how it was very important not to miss a last train, and what to do if you did. If they'd told us at Maidstone I'd have known.

Love

H

From ANNE   10 Warwick Avenue
Monday, 1 February 1943

Darling Heywood,

Went to the shop in a taxi this morning at about 11.30, and found I quite enjoyed being there – everything seemed to be all right and looking very nice; there had been no collecting so Nancy had succeeded in making Jimmy dust and tidy all morning; and it

103 Heywood is slightly mis-remembering a popular song of the time which began:

> You are my sunshine, my only sunshine,
> You make me happy when skies are grey.
> You'll never know, dear, how much I love you,
> So please don't take my sunshine away.

104 Roger Hinks (1910–63). Art historian and author of books on Carolingian art and Caravaggio; assistant keeper of the Department of Greek and Roman Antiquities at the British Museum, from which he was unfairly forced to resign as a result of a public scandal about the cleaning of the Elgin Marbles. Subsequently British Council – Rome, Amsterdam, Athens and Paris. He was a friend of Nancy who used to call him the Turkish Lady, because he used to sit on the balcony in Athens and, like a Turkish lady, watch the world go by.

105 Derek Hill (see Appendix).

looked really beautiful – still lots of piles but all moved into symmetrical positions, and a wonderful lack of dust.

I did very little work – what with Biddy and Fidelity[106] coming in – and then not being able to resist talking a lot with Nancy. I must try and remember some of the interesting and funny things she told me to tell you when I see you. I did send off about 6 *Clique* books that had accumulated – also sent off about 6 reports of books I'd marked in last week's *Clique* (I'd marked about 15 I vaguely thought we'd got, but could only find 6). I would very much like you to make a little glossary of reporting terms (fine, very fine, etc.) as I find myself at a great loss in attempting to describe things for reports. For instance, that *Canadian Scenery* with a beautiful cover – how would you describe it? Nancy said, 'Blue calf heavily gilt', but I didn't feel that was quite right; but it may be. Then some shop wanted early juvenile games, so I tried to describe some of ours, but got tremendously bogged – the report looked like one of Bason's[107] by the time I'd done.

The ordering is really too too difficult now. I suppose it is no worse than when you were here – but what *is* one to do to avoid missing things if travellers don't call? And once books are missed they're so often missed for ever, and that *is* so shaming – *never* to have some very good new book, or best-seller, at all.

Nancy now implores me to give her *all* the ordering to do, so I am going to, with the greatest pleasure. She's now evolved a very clever system – I gave her a new, much larger 'What is it' book, and she puts the name of every new book ordered that's not immediately obtainable in this 'What is it' book under the publisher (with who it's for), so that every time she has to ring up any publisher about anything she looks in this book and is reminded to jog them about all the other binding or reprinting books we want from them. I think it's really very clever of her to have thought of it.

Mollie is now doing all the day book entering (into the ledger), and the till, and says she thinks that when this lot of bills is done she won't have enough to do. So that is wonderful, and I shall gradually give her the banking, the wages, and the casebook, ending up, as my accouchement approaches, with all the invoices and the paying of the bills.

106 Biddy Harrisson and Fidelity Cranbrook (see Appendix).
107 Fred Bason, owner of the Greyhound Bookshop. His catalogues were extremely wordy.

I feel sure that you must have been having exactly the same illness as me only have not been able to indulge it as I did. It seems to have got better at exactly the same moment as mine. I feel a different person now and I hope you do too.

I have arranged to go to Ham Spray. I rang up tonight. They haven't got a cook, but *really* seemed to want me to go nevertheless. (I gave them every opportunity to say no.) So I think I shall – I thought I'd *try* to get a cold cooked chicken and other things if I possibly can, so that there would be really no cooking for at least one meal. They are looking up trains and buses to Amesbury, and if they are *impossible* they'll ring me up. If they are possible, I'm going on Thursday by a 1.45 train.

Your letter was very fascinating about all the people. It doesn't sound (comparatively) too bad. (I'm not stopping pitying you though.)

I bought a rather horrid camel-hair maternity loose three-quarter-length jacket from someone for £1 (no coupons). Very economical, but I shall feel rather horrible in it and degraded I fear. I might bring it for the weekend and see what you think.

Poor Mummy is very miserable because Vicki[108] has been missing for two days. Also she is very unhappy about Aunt Janie.

Much love

ANNE

From HEYWOOD · Larkhill
Sunday, 31 January [posted later]

Darling,

I've found a nice hotel in Amesbury – the Avon. I booked you a room Sat and Sun. Might it be a good idea if – instead of going down to Ham, you come here for Fri or Thurs and Fri as well? I shouldn't be able to get off all the nights, but it seemed a comfortable hotel, and you wouldn't have all that extra travelling to do. I gather from Derek [Hill] that Ham is a difficult journey from here. If you do think that is a good idea let me know by return so that I can book the room.

---

108 Vicki – one of her two dachshunds. They often went hunting, causing great anxiety.

You go to Salisbury. Take a taxi from the station to the bus station where you get the bus for Amesbury.

Be v. careful this week because it'll tire you starting work. *V. important* I think.

Love
H

From HEYWOOD   Larkhill
Monday 1st and Tuesday 2 February

Darling,

Fascinating letter from you today. With so much news that left me gasping. It really is sad about Aunt J. Everyone will say what a wonderful way to die. I feel sad and you'll feel very sad. Awful that you should have more cause to cry. What blubberers we'll become.

Thanks for the parcel – brilliant of you. If there are little beginners' books on trigonometry and logarithms could you bring. The easiest way would be just to ring up Foyles and let Jimmy buy them from there. But nothing at all big or expensive, and it doesn't matter much as it'll bore me frightfully to read them.

The first full day is over. First a lecture by officer. Then PT. That was unpleasant. Goes on longer than at Maidstone. They all dash in and start hurling footballs. I wish it was all exercises. Then the horse – jumping it. I floundered over. Then doing a running somersault over it. I noticed the old parson always moving to the end of the line of people who had done it – so I did that too. Another lecture. In the afternoon gun drill. We had to pull out one of those huge cannons from a shed, were shown how it worked – then in teams of sixes made to do the drill for it.

Then a lecture on a wildly complicated instrument called the Director, which old boys say is a vital thing to know about. I feel I never shall, and all the others are brilliant. Then a lecture on gas by the sergeant. He asked me what reactions I would have if the enemy used gas. I said I shouldn't like it much. Quite the wrong answer – should have said that with my present knowledge and equipment it was nothing to worry about. After that he kept asking me questions and I was extremely silly and bad. What does it matter, but it's depressing to be so bad. I get paralysed when asked questions and sink into a pit of 'Misunderstood'. The one nice moment is when the lights go out at night, and one can't be seen any more. The beginning of each day is ghastly. Oh dear. I mustn't go wailing on. I'm going to write resolutely flippant letters to Malcolm [Bullock] – about one a fortnight. Exciting about Mrs Kentall. My wretched torch keeps going out, and at night one is absolutely blind, and I have to get up in the dark not to get left behind.

I'm sure that this thing isn't my right thing. In the heat of action I could never work out a mathematical problem – even if I ever ordinarily could.

Later

Another letter from you. The letters were brought in during a lecture and laid on a bench, and I was sure there was one from you on the top, and so it was.

One tremendous thing of here is not having to do blanco. There is sort of homework to do – entering up notes in a big notebook.

Bring warm things if you can for weekend. I shall have to leave about 8.30 in the evening which is a bore. Bus goes at 9. It's a rather Orchard-like[109] sort of hotel with a drawing room.

Don't come by too late a train. If you have any troubles in Salisbury ring up Vivian Macan. Take a taxi from the station to the bus station. They say if there isn't one at once you can't have to wait long. The hotel is called the Avon (at Amesbury).

Lots of love
HEYWOOD

From ANNE   Tuesday, 2 February. In shop
Darling Heywood,

I've got your letter about arrangements. If you think you could get off in the evening I'll come on Friday. I think though that I'd better still go to Ham Spray for Thursday as I've asked myself – and evidently there must be some fairly easy way to Amesbury from there as they haven't telephoned saying don't come. Do you think you could possibly ring me up at Ham Spray on Thursday if you *can* get a room on Friday? Inkpen 204. If you don't ring up I'll come Sat.

109 The kind of hotel his parents would have liked, with what they called 'nice' people in it.

[83]

No time to write more – all's well here and I'm feeling quite recovered.

Fondest love from
ANNE

I would *prefer* to come Fri, if I would be able to see you.

[Undated draft of telegram from Anne]
Ignore my letter will come Amesbury Thursday am very sad missing you telephoning but had to wait for Sternsons longing to see you love Anne

The long weekend at Amesbury came off, Thursday 4th to Monday 8th.

From OSBERT SITWELL   Renishaw
                                   Thursday, [probably 4 February]
My dear Anne,
    I've never written to you, but I really have been ill; which has been a great bore, and I'm supposed to write no letters and stay as much as possible in bed. My heart started to behave oddly, and I had to have every sort of diagram and photograph of it – and now I'm told that it has always been like this! However, I feel better though tired. It's just this *appalling* war, and all the misery of it, a second time, too.
    Will you give my love to Heywood. Tell him he must come up *on leave* between the 10th and 20th, when I shall be in London.
    The enclosed cheque is not *just* a cheque: it's a wood of beech trees and silver birch. Just think of that when you cash it.[110]
    I do hope you are not doing too much work? What is the new girl like?

Yours ever
OSBERT

Will you credit me with 8/6 in hand for the 2nd copy of *Not Me, Sir*.

110 He'd sold a wood.

From ANNE   10 Warwick Avenue
                                             Monday, 8 February

Darling Heywood,

I wonder how you got on today at Larkhill. I expect you had a
horrible day. I thought of you a lot there.

My start at Amesbury was successful. The maid never called me
though told to, but I miraculously awoke from profound sleep at 25
past 7. I got to the bus stop so early that I caught the bus before the
right one, so arrived at Andover about ½ past 9, after a nice pretty
drive, rather desecrated by 100s and 100s of rifle etc ranges. Confusion and contradiction amongst porters about whether the train
was 10.08 or 10.20. I got into one about 10 past 10 which arrived at
½ past 11, better than ours.

Shop pretty awful. Seemed somehow to be tremendous number
of books wanted and to be looked up, and letters to be answered
and urgent bills to pay, and receipts to do; and too many interruptions ever to get anything much done

Osbert's paid his £80 which is good.

Mollie says she really would like to do more, and can, so I'm
going to show her about the banking and wage-paying.

It was lovely being at Amesbury for so long. I enjoyed the
Stonehenge Larkhill morning very much.

Try not to get too crushed and depressed by it all – though it
must be almost impossible not to be. But when the pressure is
removed you will rise again.

That airman runner came in today, and I am rather pleased as I
bought about 80 sheets of that engraved writing paper from him. I
also bought an album of about 90 postcards of pre-last-war actors
and actresses. I am posting the 2 best to Osbert and Frances.

I am getting into terrible confusion over those unmarked
Valentines.

                                                      Morning
Late – posting this on way to shop.

                                                      Love
                                                         A

From FRANCES PARTRIDGE   Ham Spray House
                                            Marlborough
                                                  Wilts
                                        Monday, 8 February

My dear Anne,

We were disappointed indeed not to see you – but very glad that
the reason of it was your going straight to Amesbury and not some
disaster or other. On the whole it sounds better for H there – *hellish*
though it must be in all circumstances. I feel that for him and him
alone we shall get an icy flood of realistic light thrown upon that
horrible institution – the Army I mean. But the war surely must
come to an end now, how can it go on?

I suppose Heywood couldn't hitch hike over here? And you
could meet for a weekend here or something? We studied the means
of transport, which do not seem impossible, though of course
maddeningly complex. From Julia and L's[111] village 2 miles off
there is a bus to Andover, and one takes a train from there to
Amesbury (changing I believe at Porton, a tiny station so it can't be
a bad change). The trouble is the bus only runs certain days, but Fri
and Sat are both all right. So if you can ever manage it again *do* –
by leaving here 11 something you get there 2 something. Not bad.

R. says he will send off the books.

We have heard no more news about Rollo.[112] I wonder if there is
any. I hope Janetta and K[113] are coming next weekend – and we
shall hear if there is then. Any fine fat nannies blown along? What
about a coal-black Mammy?

We have been suffering rather here from both our henchmen,
gardener and char, having heart attacks. I'm afraid it doesn't speak
very well for our services, and we always flatter ourselves we are
wildly indulgent employers. They totter back from time to time and
do a little feeble work.

I think it's monstrous making the poor married women who do
all the work of their houses do munitions as well. Poor Julia has
been pounced on as a mobile woman, and had to go off to another
interview, but she managed wonderfully and has got a 6-month

---

111 Julia Strachey and Lawrence Gowing who lived together at Lambourn. They later
got married.
112 Rollo Woolley. He was Janetta's brother, missing in North Africa.
113 Kenneth Sinclair-Loutit and Janetta Woolley (see Appendix).

extension to finish her 'novel' – 'not an ordinary novel, you know, but a novel with a *message*'.[114] Rather a brilliant touch that.

Well must stop now. Do let us know at *any* time if you can come here – and Heywood too if he could get here. No news yet of R's appeal,[115] but he is collecting magnificent testimonials as some people collected stamps. The last is from an ambassador – that ought to fetch them.

Much love from us both and we hope to see you soon. Might we I wonder stop the night with you when R's appeal comes on?

Yr. FRANCES

From HEYWOOD   Larkhill
                                                   Monday, 8 February
Darling,

This morning I was sent for and shown a letter from the War Office saying I'd been sent here by mistake and was wanted by the Intelligence. I was given a form to full in with my particulars, the reason why I wanted to transfer, and so on. I filled it in and that's all so far. It was only a clerk I saw. I asked how long it would be before I was transferred but he didn't know.

Quite likely it'll only be another frying pan (today I heard of a specialist who has just finished his course saying that he was being sent to the Intelligence somewhere near Sheffield) but still it's somehow very cheering.

I thought of you in all your stages today – the tipping – the bus and the train. I longed to be looking after you. I hope it wasn't too awful. It was a very nice little interlude, wasn't it – though it seemed to evaporate in no time. It's always so dreadful leaving you.

It wasn't too bad today. I was asked by the officer if I was 'all-at-sea' about the Director. I didn't have the courage to say yes. Very foolish.

I took the gym vest this morning belonging to the same man whose coat I took, and I found I'd put his in my kitbag. He's

114 Julia's 'novel'. This didn't really exist, according to Frances Partridge, except insofar as she was always working on a hundred things at this time. The chief thing was a play about an ice mountain, with the main character being a cricket, something Julia insisted was simple to stage. See also *Julia* by Frances Partridge, London, 1983.
115 Ralph Partridge, a convinced pacifist, was appealing against being made to serve in the Home Guard. See Frances Partridge's *A Pacifist's War*.

wonderfully tolerant, and so far hasn't called me a fucking cunt. I try to appease him with Aunt Dorothy's cake.

I've exhausted my letter writing today by writing to Sheila[116] to thank her for the pullover. It's much colder today. Don't send the pyjamas if you haven't already, in case I move. I imagine the very earliest would be a week, as this form will have to filter through.

Much much love. I love you more and more. Wouldn't Mama help you in the shop on Friday? When I got back last night I read a chapter of *War and Peace* and there was a bit, 'the little princess looked up with that curious expression of inner happy calm peculiar to pregnant women'. I then thought that I'd seen that expression on you. So you see Frances is right and you are like that – even if you don't think you feel it. Be horrid to customers on Tuesday. But you won't get this till Wed.

I tried to ring tonight but two hours delay. That fat man – the one who was at the hotel and you thought I meant was at Eton with me – was in the NAAFI tonight and he talked to me and said 'Rather different to last night.' He said he'd been trying for the Intelligence but was too old. He said he was at Winchester and the first 6 months was hard but after that v. nice.

H

From ANNE 10 Warwick Avenue
Tuesday, 9 February

Darling Heywood,

I found the most *wonderful* present from you when I got back this evening.[117] It was the surprise of my life and most exciting, in a registered parcel. It really is lovely and I am very pleased with it. I couldn't think how you could possibly have got it, and then I remembered, I suppose it was through the Indian. I wonder if you saw the box, as I think it is very pretty, rich and distinguished looking; it looks like a real grey lizardskin.

John and Sheila [Hill] are here tonight for the night. It's now ½ past 11. So I must stop and sleep, and tomorrow there's going to be too much to do too early for me to write, so this will have to be

116 Sheila Hill (see Appendix).
117 It was their fifth wedding anniversary. The present was a box of make-up things, very difficult to get at that time.

very short. And tomorrow is my Ina[118] evening, so if I write one at all, it will be short too I fear.

One thing, Mrs Kentall rang up tonight and is coming – she's got a doctor's certificate saying she must not do factory work or any purely indoor work, and must if possible be in the open air for a part of the day, as she's had lung trouble. She says not to do anything about the Labour Exchange, and I expect she's right. She's coming Monday week, and Jimmy's medical's this Friday, and the arrangement with him is, if he's A1 he's leaving Wednesday so we'll have 3 days with no one, if he's any other grade he's staying till Saturday. I had rather a row with him again this morning, as he arrived at nearly ½ past 10 – I said things like 'It's not fair to me when everything's difficult enough for me as it is with Mr Hill away'. I also said – I started with 'It's very *silly* of you to work so badly for us, as after the war what sort of reference shall we be able to give you?' He said, 'I shall stay in the Forces – I shan't go back to civvy life.'[119] I felt annoyed with myself afterwards as it was all so futile, but he does arouse such rage in me.

I asked Mrs Kentall if she'd mind sometimes being in the shop at lunch time, and she said, 'Oo I should *love* it.' I must have the talk with Smith now.

The baby is moving so terrifically just now that one can see it's heaving about through the bedclothes. I believe it is a good sign and means it will be a fine lively child.

It is awful I have no present for you, and that I didn't send you a wire, and you didn't have a letter even.

ANNE

From HEYWOOD   Larkhill
                                                      Tuesday, 9 February
Darling Anne,
    Feeling rather low tonight sitting in the NAAFI reading room – which is cold. Have just had some nasty ham and egg pie and a

118 Ina, daughter of Charles Sawyer, in whose bookshop Heywood had worked for seven years. It was she who first gave him the idea of starting a bookshop of his own, and she helped Anne enormously in its early stages, over the accounts, about the ways of various publishers' 'trade departments', what to do about customers who never paid – and many other things. She was tiny, delightful, and became a close friend of them both.
119 He liked the Navy, did stay in after the war, and became a petty officer.

bit of ginger cake. But there was fried egg for breakfast yesterday morning, and they gave one a bar of chocolate at tea time. The NAAFI chocolate is rather a swindle this week. A mucky sort of choc-tof sandwich.

I told a man about my possible transfer, who said it might be 3 or 4 weeks before it came through.

An officer made a sort of appeal today for volunteers for the paratroops. A man's job, he said, nothing pansy about it – and no glamour boys wanted, and the average of casualties only slightly higher than motor bicyclists.

We began logarithms this morning. I more or less understood. A letter from Malcolm who'd had an hour's drink with Jim [McKillop] in Sloane Square. I keep stopping and going into a blank, so I shall sink into *War and Peace* for half an hour before walking to that pillar box with this mingy letter, and then bed – wonderful bed.

Love
HEYWOOD

From HEYWOOD   Larkhill
Thursday, 11 February

Darling Anne,

This is 7.30 a.m. in the dorm. 'You're a fast mover this morning' – the youth above me has just said. I haven't swept under the bed which I ought to have done. It's difficult to snatch the broom, and the bristles are off it. Being a specialist in the dorm is rather like being a Tug at Eton.[120] The ordinary gunners feel towards them the same mixture of angry awe and contempt. There have been a few dangerous moments but no explosions yet. The youths pull each other out of bed and have fights. Luckily I'm not very near the most violent ones. I appease the nearest ones with bits of cake.

Now it's the evening of the next day. I took this to the Sunday Times reading room to finish, and found my pen had run out, and I've been thwarted ever since. The ST Reading Room isn't at all bad. A fire, and hung with 'contemporary lithographs' (you know – like we had in the shop).

Two letters from you which was wonderful. I'm so glad the

120 A scholar in College.

[90]

present arrived. I thought it might not, as I still haven't heard from the Indian. I haven't seen it and had no idea what it would be like – except that he said it was Jane Seymour.[121] You mustn't lose it before I see it.

We had to go on a route march this morning. 10 miles. Coming back was agony, and my feet are a mass of blisters. This afternoon was a football match, but I managed to be a looker-on again.

I'll book you a room at the Avon for weekend after this one. There's a dim chance I could get a sleeping-out pass – very dim. Don't come if Saunders is at all doubtful about the travelling. What with all that thudding and kicking mightn't it be coming sooner than we think?

It seems as if Harriet[122] is going to be a sort of Roedean girl. Whatever shall we do to protect ourselves from her?

That personal letter was from Frances Hendry.[123] She says about me in the Army – 'Let yourself be engulfed without horror – because if you do it will be all right. There are more ways than one of interpreting 'he that loseth his life shall find it'. I think that she will have to be made to join up with Duncan and Jimmy. How splendid about Mrs K. I wonder if you have faced up to Smith? Very difficult and dreadful. But weren't you going to wait till after Mrs K. had been a bit?

Frances's letter was interesting (of course). I feel put dreadfully on my mettle by her saying that only from me will they get a clear cold description of the Army. I think she said that – I've left the letter. I shall think a lot about that, and it will take a week to write the letter. I shan't write to you at all except a copy but I shan't of course really achieve it.

Love – my darling – very soon you'll be able to have longer and longer lapses from the shop and to fold yourself in the pregnant serenity and to damn all.

H

---

121 The firm that made the make-up.
122 Anne and Heywood had already taken the rather risky steps of deciding both the sex and the name of Anne's baby.
123 A middle-aged friend, more Heywood's than Anne's.

From ANNE   Tudor[124]
                                       Shepherd's Market
                                    Thursday, 11 February
Darling H,

This is Mollie's day off but Nancy's kindly come for lunch, too late to queue at the hostel.) How *wonderful* about the Intelligence. I am very excited. Even if you get sent to Sheffield or Scotland I still think it *must* be much better not to be a gunner – I do think it *must* really happen now, though it could take ages.

Osbert came in and was rather splendid – bought everything he looked at without looking at it properly – something I'd bought from Merino yesterday for £2 and had felt uneasy about I sold him for £4 and another Merino thing I grossly profiteered over by a mistake – £1. 2. 6 and I sold it to O. for £5 – I think I'll have to say a bit less as it's really rather a shabby rotten old thing.

Rather wonderful Smith news I went down to the packing room yesterday and told him Mrs Kentall was coming full time and going to help upstairs a bit too – then my courage failed me and I couldn't say anything else. Then I noticed he was trying to say something in an embarrassed way himself – and it turns out that he *wants* to leave; he would never have mentioned it but he thought if Mrs Kentall was coming ... They want him at that select bridge club where Mrs Smith works. He's going to find out about the wages and conditions.

Brian Howard[125] came in on Mollie's Tuesday off and stayed nearly all day reading. He was very nice. We talked off and on between his looking at books and reading them and my working, and I was pleased because after a bit it became as if he was a very old friend, whereas really, although I have seen him every now and then for a long time, it's always been as Eddie's friend – have never had a conversation with him by myself before. He'd come up on a day's leave and had got Pierre Lansel[126] to sign a certificate saying he was ill – he was rather frightened when I told him about your CB. He paid for the Christmas cards.

124 Café in Shepherd's Market.
125 A close friend of Eddie Gathorne-Hardy. A poet and, in his youth during the 1920s, an extravagant member of the aesthete-homosexual circle at Oxford. A wit, notorious for outrageous behaviour and remarks. He once, in uniform, gave his name as 'Mrs Brown' to a colonel of the Military Police. In later years, drink and drugs led to bouts of despair, in one of which he killed himself.
126 Swiss doctor who lived in England.

Must stop and go back.

Devoted love from
ANNE

PS That case has got some lovely things in it that I haven't been able to get at all for some time. Rouge for instance.

Jock[127] came in yesterday, and Aunt Janie's 'wishes' were her pearl necklace to Biddy,[128] and £50 to each of her godchildren, of which I was not one. I had *faintly* hoped for something like £5, or even £50, but not enough to be shockingly disappointed. (Granny left me £5, which made me think she might.)

I'm afraid I've done a dreadful thing – I've eaten all the month's chocolate ration in two days. But it was only double what we had at Amesbury – I took it in chocolate peppermint creams, and yesterday there was nothing to eat at tea, and I was going to the play with Ina before having dinner, so I had a lot, and the day before I was alone and had sandwiches in the shop and ate a lot, and today I just couldn't stop myself from eating all the rest.

Will tell you about Ina tonight.

You needn't sent back the Hodgson catalogue as I've got another.

From ANNE   Thursday, 11 February

Darling Heywood,

Having dinner at the Marble Arch Lyons.[129] It is rather nice really with the music playing. The only thing is I feel you are sure to be ringing up Warwick Ave. I worked till 8.30 tonight; don't worry though as I feel very well; though busy it was rather a good day at the shop. Osbert came in; he was very nice, extremely concerned about you (as he always is). He says now his heart is bad. It evidently really must be rather bad I think, as he seems to be going to a lot of specialists and doesn't look very well. He was very excited by the engraved letters I'd got from the Airman, wants to send one of each to 3 lots of people (I said he could have them cheaper if he got a lot).

Must go or there'll be no buses.

127 Jock Cranbrook (see Appendix).
128 Anne's first cousin Bridget D'Oyly Carte (1909–85). She had been Jock's first wife: they married in 1926 and divorced in 1931.
129 Mrs Sternson cooked for Anne five nights a week. On the nights she didn't Anne usually ate out so as not to be in their way in the kitchen.

Mrs Ionides[130] sent someone for the musical box today so it really was a good day – makes up for some horrid failures I've had that I haven't told you about.

I've told Mr Merino I've asked you about 2 books days ago, and I haven't really. *The Capitals of Europe 1814*, complete (he lays stress on that) £12 in v. good condition. I'm very inclined to get that without waiting for your answer, for Osbert – fired by my successes. *Complete Works of Verlaine* 2 vols. 1902 £3.10/-.

Mummy's not coming for the weekend after all which is rather sad. Franzel[131] has got distemper very badly, and the maids can't look after him (it is like pneumonia; it all depends on the nursing).

If you were at Sheffield it wouldn't be so bad – you could go to Renishaw, and there's sure to be a very good train service from London.

Fondest love from

ANNE

From HEYWOOD   Larkhill
Friday, 12 February

Darling Anne,

This can only be a scrap. Derek [Hill] is coming over tonight. Just got your letter. It all seems to be fitting in splendidly about the Smiths.

I think it's easier to send you back the Hodgson catalogue. Nos. 144, 145, 241 are only tentative, if Nancy thinks they're very nice, and if you think we can afford them. Some of them sound Osbert-like. (You could fix a limit to what she'd spend altogether.)

Remember to send Mr Osborne[132] 10/-.

Nothing new from here. I'm in great confusion with the trig. and logs. I find a lot of the others are policemen – of the hearty uppish sort. Beastly gun drill now – but then the weekend. I shall go to have a bath at Fighting Cocks[133] this evening.

Love

H

130 A figure in the museum world, wife of a rich Greek collector.
131 Another of her dachshunds. Anne's mother always had long-haired dachshunds. Franzel had other things wrong with him. He grew hugely fat and his hair frizzled up into tight curls.
132 Of Hodgsons. Anyone who could not go to the sale could leave bids with him.
133 A nearby house where friends of Heywood's parents lived, Joan and Torquil MacNeil.

6.30, Friday, 12 February

Darling Heywood,

Not a nice day at all today. I feel wretchedly miserable and long for you. All the usual silly little things – lost my 'What is it' book, so now don't know where to send all the books that have arrived. I had to go to the doctor this morning, and thought the appointment was at quarter past 11 so that I'd just have time to read the letters here and Smith[134] everything before going to him, but it was a quarter to, so I had to go straight from home. And though Jimmy's medical was at 8 a.m. he never came all day. So the last chance of collecting before Monday has gone. So today I have looked up and either Smithed or rung up the publishers of 40 books (I've just counted). Well, some of them I looked up yesterday, but they've all still got to be got and sent. There's also a fearful clip of unanswered letters I can't manage to get seen to.

Home having supper

Nice concert now. But I'll still go on telling you how horrid the shop was. While I was seeing Saunders *of course* the Allen & Unwin, Longman and Macmillan travellers all came in; the Macmillan one especially I've been longing to see for weeks.

Also while I was out Osbert came in. I'd spent about an hour at least yesterday sorting out the beastly engraved letters, and had written him a note about them in case I was out. He was apparently appalled at the price they worked out at – said they would be at half a crown each and that he remembered them when they were not much more expensive than ordinary writing paper. And is not having them of course. I now feel I *have* been grossly over-charging for them (though I did make the reduction I said I would in my last letter from £7. 6. 0. to £5. 10. 0. What do *you* think? Do say, will you please?

The doctor as usual was very pleased with me. Listened to the baby's heart through an instrument. I had been having cramp in my legs; he says that is from the baby pressing on a nerve that connects with my legs, and that it means it is low down, which is a very good thing for the birth.

Roger Fulford[135] came again. He obviously really is Roger Fulford

134 To order from W. H. Smith.
135 Sir Roger Fulford (1902–83). Liberal politician and author. Books included *Royal Dukes*, 1933; *Queen Victoria*, 1951; *The Trial of Queen Caroline*, 1967.

as he was getting books for his stepson who was just back wounded from Libya. He was very nice and said what a good collection of new books we'd got, and how the Oxford bookshops had got nothing.

I've done none of the things you wanted me to do like ringing up Shemilt [picture framer]. And as for paying the rest of the bills, I haven't begun. And the January little men[136] are still not paid. Another worry is Nancy's doctor says she's anaemic, and must have a lot of fresh air and exercise. I said emphatically she *must* have a holiday next week too, but it will be very difficult without her.

Jan[137] has been taken to the Paddington hospital very seriously ill today, some sort of lung thing - not pneumonia. Trachea . . . what is that? I hope to God she's not going to die. I was going to ask her to tea on Sunday.

I'm sorry to go droning on and on and *on* like this in such a dreary way, But you won't be getting the letter till Monday and by then I'm sure to be feeling quite different, so you needn't worry.

Sunday lunchtime
Had lunch with Sheila and Biddy [Harrisson] yesterday (Biddy was entirely a mistake – however *she* gave *us* lunch at Gunters and me 6/- change as well. Couldn't go on and on for *ever* giving it back to her.) Coney[138] had given me a half bottle of Portuguese brandy which Sheila and I half finished in the shop before lunch. After closing we had a late lunch.

Jimmy had never come at all. I feel furious and despairing. But Smith did come and was very nice and paternal, and I think rather embarrassed about Jimmy. He packed and posted everything.

After the lunch I came back to the shop, tidied it a bit, and then sat in the armchair and read and slept for about an hour without working. Then I walked to Sloane Square, dropping a parcel on

---

136 The 'little men' whom Anne tried to pay promptly were the small booksellers, many of whom lived precariously on a razor's edge of alternating overdrafts and too small bank balances. Though G. Heywood Hill's premises at 17 Curzon Street looked imposing (they were much larger than those at No. 10 now) the shop too was in much the same situation. The publishers mostly had to be paid monthly, whereas Anne only managed to get the shop's own bills sent out every three or four months – and many customers were extremely dilatory over paying them even when they did arrive. Even when on paper the shop might seem to be doing well there was a perpetual cash shortage.
137 Jan Woolley (see Appendix).
138 Coney Jarvis, wife of Ralph Jarvis, Anne's cousin.

Eddie Sackville-West[139] on the way, bussed along the King's Road and had tea with Jim [Lees-Milne][140] at Cheyne Walk. It is an *extremely* nice house; wonderful position, right on a bend of the river, so that from the sitting room you have a view of the river in two directions. He seemed to be happy and enjoying it all – the view and his dachshund and the tea. I enjoyed them all too – it was rather wonderful after the bad days at the shop. He did the tea himself – toast and golden syrup which I hadn't had for ages.

He said gratifying things about the shop, how very *established* it was now and how everybody regarded it as a centre, and arranged to meet there, and how *constantly* people said how good it was, and that last week he heard two people talking about it, one of whom knew it and the other didn't, and the one who knew it was saying how good it was, and the other one said, 'But it's a very small shop, isn't it?' and the first one said, 'Yes, but they have a very good selection of books, and anything they haven't got they'll always get for you' (hardly true, I fear). Those sort of things make me feel one *ought* to go on having new books always, as well as old, despite the great bother of them.[141]

After lunch, Warwick Avenue
Delightful music on the Forces Programme – I wonder if you're listening to it too, ('Loch Lomond' and now 'Johnny Cannuck's Revue') in the Sunday Times Reading Room, which sounds very nostalgic with its contemporary lithographs. I feel very sad, long for you, and the 'Bluebells of Scotland'. After the war if one can't get abroad we might go to some of the Islands – I'd love to do that. I'd like to see all the places I used to go to again too, and the people.

I *did* ask the doctor about travelling – he said next weekend would be *quite* all right (I was truthful and described the bus ride

139 Eddie Sackville-West (1901–65). Novelist, critic and musician, he succeeded Lord Sackville in 1962. He was one of that distinguished literary, musical and artistic group who shared Long Crichel House in Dorset. Besides Eddie, this comprised Eardley Knollys, the painter, Desmond Shawe-Taylor, the music critic, and the literary critic Raymond Mortimer, who joined them later.
140 James Lees-Milne (b. 1908). Architectural historian, biographer and diarist. National Trust Historic Buildings Committee Secretary 1936–51, and architectural adviser 1951–66. Once engaged to Anne, he married Alvilde Chaplin in 1936. This encounter with Anne is recalled in his *Ancestral Voices*.
141 Heywood sometimes thought, longingly, that it would be nice only to sell old books, perhaps by catalogue, from a house in the country.

etc.). He said for a month from the 27th I should be careful as it is a tricky time for some reason. He was much less fussy though this time, and seemed to think I could go on at the shop more or less, off and on, right up to the last fortnight – I suppose I must be more well than he expected me to be – and indeed I *am* well. He says I should go to Ronans[142] about 17 April. I have the tel. no. of an ambulance place who will rush me down to Windsor at a moment's notice if I start the baby too soon, here in London.

Now a lovely Rossini-Mozart concert on the Home programme, How cruel that they don't turn that on ever; couldn't you get at the wireless somehow – no, I suppose not.

I must stop writing to you and do some work – extremely loath though I am. Jimmy is not coming next week at all! Never again in fact. He is going into hospital on Monday to have his rupture rectified, and then will be accepted for the Navy. Smith at least has 'let me know' – he left a message with Mrs Sternson last night, with some ledgers I'd asked him to bring. Fortunately, Nancy is coming next week, and says she is feeling much better; so I have been through all the list of books wanted, and have boiled down the urgent collections to about 5, and am sending orders by post from the duplicate book for all the rest, including stock orders from the *Times Literary Sup.* and *Observer*. I have written on each order 'If not in stock, please place on order. If unobtainable kindly let me know.' It will be interesting and useful to see what happens. All the ones that haven't answered or sent by Friday I shall ring up.

Am *longing* for the next weekend. Do try hard for a sleeping-out pass. It would be wonderful.

Fondest fondest love from
ANNE

From HEYWOOD   Larkhill
Saturday, 13 February

Darling Anne,

I *may* be going over to lunch at Ham Spray on Sunday. If I can get to Ludgershall Michael McCarthy[143] will drive me over. It depends whether I can get a train – there are no buses in the morning. I shan't be able to post you a letter till Tues. as I have to do the

142 The Lambes' house near Bracknell.
143 Michael, son of the critic Desmond McCarthy.

telephone business on Monday night. Michael and Derek [Hill] came over last night. Derek said it was a triumph for Michael coming. He always wanted to go to places but could never start. Once we had started the Partridge idea he was full of agitations about the means and the ringings up. Derek was rung up twice during dinner.

I had a maddening little packet from Daddy today. I thought it was chocolate but it was only throat pastilles – with a letter to ask what had he said before about money? Neither he nor mother could remember. He knows he said he would give £50 towards the doctor but couldn't remember anything else. I shall write back and tell him straight – but it's rather agitating.

I do hope my transfer comes through before my bewilderment over all I'm supposed to be learning is shown up. There's an exam in 2 weeks' time.

I'm just starting off for 'Fighting Cocks' – and then the Aunts[144] – half hoping to be asked to dinner.

The youths are very wild this afternoon and I keep having to step over fighting heaps. It's lucky you sewed on those buttons. The others are pouring off. Perhaps Frances will do some.

Malcolm has sent me £1 with an illegible letter full of jokes about baby clothes. How boring for you Mama not coming. I shan't ring up – unless my transfer comes through or something. There always seems to be two hours' delay.

I'm now in the Avon. They've consented to keep you a room for Sat. and Sun. – after a lot of dotty red tape about writing to confirm it. I wish I hadn't said about a pass as I now think it's extremely unlikely. Don't come if you in the least feel not up to the effort. I'm hoping that in the transfer we'll manage another meeting.

I think I should get the Verlaine from Merino. I don't know about *The Capitals of Europe*. Don't know it. If it's coloured, if you haven't seen it I should make him show it to you first; it might be hideous. How splendidly you're doing with Osbert. Malcolm writes scathingly about Osbert.

My boots were found to be dirty on parade this morning. No results except a public explosion.

Now I really must go to Fighting Cocks.

Love

H

144 John Hill's aunts: Mrs Ethel Bailey and Phyllis, widow of Major-General Walker Pitts Hendy Hill, CB, CMG, DSO, who had been killed a few months earlier.

PS A very boring thing, but I told a man I'd try to get him *Teach Yourself German*. It's one of those Hodder horrors (which calls itself English University Press). I told him it was probably impossible, but would you have one shot. If you come next weekend, try to get here for lunch.

From ANNE   Monday, 15.2.43.
Darling Heywood,
    Only time for a scrap, as it's in the Hostel and a quarter past 2.
    It's very said about Jan, isn't it? I found though that it wasn't a shock and I felt nothing. It *was* pneumonia – I'll tell you all about it when I see you.
    Jane[145] is spending the night tonight (Francis's firewatching night).
    Osbert came in this morning, and said he'd come to apologise for being so mean about the engraved letters, a great relief. On the other hand I bought that Merino book – I couldn't resist it. It was the *Triumphs of Europe* – not the same copy as before, and bound in with it was an extra thing – the *Something of Waterloo*, with a lot more colour plates. He said £12 but of course then an extra 21/- had to be given to him. I'm charging £18. Can't find it in *Book Auction Records*. Well the moment it arrived Chips [Channon][146] came in and I showed it to him. He said he'd got it – how much were we charging? When I told him he was silent. Then, I think fortunately, I was rather candid with him. I said I'd just bought it that morning, and did he think I was charging too much for it? I said, 'What did *you* pay – or I suppose I oughtn't to ask that?' This rather pleased him somehow, and he said, 'Yes, I will tell you, and I promise I won't tell anyone else – £6 just before Christmas at . . . ' I was appalled – on the other hand, I hadn't yet looked at it properly, and possibly his didn't have the supplement about Waterloo; (I'll

145 Jane, wife of Francis Watson – friends. Francis Watson (1909–92) was assistant keeper (1938–63) then director (1963–74) of the Wallace Collection. Surveyor of the Queen's Works of Art (1963–77). Knighted in 1973.
146 Sir Henry Channon (1897–1958). An American from Chicago, always known as 'Chips', who arrived in London in 1918 and rose swiftly both in society and politics. Became an MP in 1935 and PPS to Rab Butler in 1938-41. *Chips*, his candid diary, was published in 1967. Married to Lady Honor Guinness, 1933–45. Knighted in 1957. One of his purchases from the shop is recorded as being *Cautionary Tales*.

ask him). What do you think? Will you please say, and also what the engraved notepaper should cost.

Love

ANNE

10 Warwick Avenue

Monday, 15 February

10.20 p.m., in bed

Darling Heywood,

I found my letter to you about ½ an hour after the post had gone. Dropped it into letter box but too late – now fear you'll have nothing tomorrow or on Wed.

How awful about Father forgetting about our allowance. It was so *definite* wasn't it? Of course no chance we've got the letter anywhere I fear. I'm having lunch with Father on Thurs. I know I shall forget to book a table at Gunters. I don't think he wants to much but feels he ought. Poor Father.

Am liking Jane. Went to bed early all the same.

Smith didn't arrive till 20 past 4 today. He was of course only able to post 4 parcels out of 15 that should have gone, and perhaps 10 letters. He is *odd*, isn't he, though he is so nice and I am convinced fond of us, to work as little as all that – it's not the only time. Think it may be something physical, actually the matter with him.

Splendid new 36-Curzon-Street-addressed rich young sisters came in today, and in about 5 minutes bought 2 *Oxford Companion to Music*, 2 *Oxford Dictionary of Quotations*, 3 *Oxford Book of English Verse*, Osbert Lancaster's Munnings and a lot of children's books, in all about £12. We're out of all those Oxford books now, so I have already re-ordered. And they've already ordered one of the new *Oxford Book of Quotations*.

I've bought a nice small clock with dolls that dance and revolve on top, at the hour, on sale for the moment from the same place as that oil-painting doctor came from. £7. 10/-. Viva [King] came in, and I was disappointed that she didn't buy it. They are pretty dolls. The whole thing rather small, about the height of this paper. Unfortunately, it is only in rather erratic working order. The dolls stick and have to be helped. I should think it's rather early. Viva had got a wonderful musical box jewel on a sort of clip-seal, about 2 inches long, that plays a tune against one's ear.

[101]

Am staying at home tomorrow bill-paying. Rather a relief, as do feel rather tired today.

A very eventless day in the shop. My writing to publishers on Sunday was rather successful; 5 have already sent. I am carefully noting which ones do send quickly, and shall make more use of them. If only one could do nothing else, one could eventually evolve a wonderful way of getting books from the publishers and off to customers in no time, even now in the war.

Got Nancy off to Hodgsons. She was very enthusiastic, and left bids for most. We've got about £500 in the bank – will have a good deal less by the end of tomorrow though.

Had lunch with Isobel Strachey[147] which was why I couldn't finish my letter to you – I try to post my letters to you in the middle of the day now, and *not* leave them to the risks of later Smithery.

Smith is going to the Exclusive Bridge Club, either Monday or Wednesday. So now, may all be well with Mrs K. (She comes Monday unless some frightful catastrophe prevents.)

Dined with Nancy at Norway tonight. Norway as embarrassing as ever, the same tummy-patting, and saying it's a boy and that I must eat for two, very loud, and making all the room somehow participate in the remarks, and calling me Lady Anne all the time. Topolski[148] was there. The food was delicious I must say, and masses of it and very cheap, soup, lamb chops, fried potatoes, onions, and red cabbage, and coffee with cream, for 2/9.

Tomorrow I'll ring up the station about trains. I'll arrange to arrive for lunch. I suppose there can be no risk of there not being any buses from Andover? On Saturday? I'm assuming they're every half an hour, and will try to arrive at Andover about 11.30. Oh, how exciting. I must try not to forget the camera. I will put it in some prominent place tonight.

Going to bed now. Longing to get a letter from you tomorrow. Harriet is thudding away powerfully.

---

147 First wife of the painter John Strachey, Lytton's nephew. She was the daughter of a railway magnate who set up the railway in Argentina, where Isobel was brought up. She was an artist, author of numerous novels, including *A Summer in Buenos Aires*, and a woman of great charm and original wit who ran a successful small salon for many years.

148 Feliks Topolski (1907–89). Polish artist, theatrical designer and film-maker. Naturalised British in 1947.

Oh I nearly forgot to say – Jock came in today and is giving me £50! On account of Aunt Janie. So he's made it as if I was a god-child. Isn't it wonderful? We needn't feel guilty and anxious about staying in hotels now for ages.

Franzel has died, in spite of all the care and attention. I *must* write and condole to Mama tomorrow.

My Army Allowance Pay Book was at the Post Office all the time. I asked on the faint off-chance today. So like that post office not to dream of sending me a p.c. to say they'd got it – or of sending it itself (it's got my address all over it). So I got a nice lot of money from that and there's quite a lot more to come – several weeks' 9/6 for the baby on another book I hadn't got with me. Perhaps we shan't need to pay by cheque this time at the hotel.

Fondest love from

ANNE

From HEYWOOD   Larkhill
Tuesday, 16 February

Darling,

It was lovely to get your long letter today. Awful though for you all the shop agonising frets. Do go on always telling them to me.

Rather a sell in the sadistic way that Jimmy is in the Navy and not the Army.

I remember that exactly the same sort of thing happened before with Osbert over that sort of notepaper. I suppose he once bought it very cheap. You could tell him that you must have paid too much for it (though I don't think you did). I'm sure it's a good thing for stock and will sell all right in the end.

Rather a triumph getting to Ham Spray wasn't it? I was in a hereditary bus and taxi fever most of the time. I arranged for the hired car to pick me up by the church – because I didn't want to be seen stepping into it. Of course I arranged it for exactly the time of the service so that great regiments started to pour by just as I did get in. I turned up my collar and opened a paper and tried to look like a general. I had to meet Michael near a farm about a mile from Biddesden. The taxi cost 18/-. I waited in the road for ½ an hour – the Home Guard went by – before he arrived. He talked about sharing houses with people and said how intellec-tual people couldn't take others for granted but must be always dissecting them, whereas poor people accepted others and didn't bother – so long as they kept a rule of two. Michael rather implying that he was like that. I think perhaps he is but not in a simple way but in a cynical amused way. He was funny – I do like him. But I think it's nonsense what he says, because poor people dissect like mad, and only have to accept others because they can't get rid of them. (I didn't think of saying that to him.)

We got to Ham Spray about half an hour before lunch. A rather boring neighbour woman with a man came to lunch – a duty – but they didn't stay long. I was rather lumpish and sleepy and fumbling and in awe of being there and thinking of the time slipping, but I did enjoy it and it was of course wonderful to be there. The telegram about Jan came just before tea. Ralph and Michael had gone out, and Frances and I had a moment of intimate shock. They'd asked Jan to stay that weekend. Neither of us felt any immediate sadness about her. Perhaps partly because of Rollo.[149] Frances feels sad for Janetta – so many things. Ralph says it will make her money thing much worse. But it is a sad tragedy of Jan. You'll have felt it fairly strongly. The number of deaths is frightening.

By 6 Michael had shown no signs of going, so I had to do the move-making. We went to Biddesden and into the big house and Betty Guinness[150] gave us a drink. Then Derek arrived, and stayed with Betty while we went to Michael's (I had to make him go again). When we got there he drew a sheet off the table, and there was some old cheese and some cod's roe (the cod's roe was v.g. and came from Fortnum's – it would be worth you trying to get – for yourself not me). He gave me just a little cod's roe and was very pleased when I took Derek's jam. He ended by driving me to Ludgershall, where I gave him a drink, and I caught the bus to Amesbury, and *just* caught the last one from there to here, so all was well.

It's now ¼ past two in the morning. I'm on that telephone business, and have just been woken by the other man whose turn it now is to sleep under the table. Except for the sleeplessness I don't mind doing it. It's warm in the little office and peaceful. The other man is rather nice. The sort of 'bad influence' sort. Lazy and fat-faced, has been here five months, has failed once in the exam and is bitter

149 Rollo had finally been declared missing presumed dead.
150 Elisabeth, wife of Bryan Guinness, later Lord Moyne. Biddesden was their English house; they had another in Ireland.

about army life; is an obviously successful dodger. I couldn't make him talk much as he was too lazy, but there was one burst last night.

They were very nice to me at 'Fighting Cocks', and I had a wonderful bath, and she sewed on my buttons, and I stayed to dinner. The Aunts had left a message for me that they had to go out and couldn't see me and would I ring up after 10 days.

Bring rather a lot of money when you come – to pay for the hotel, and about £2 for me.

Enclosed letter is from Paul Latham.[151] So far he seems quite happily sorry for himself and undaunted – don't you think? He's evidently living on the edge of his estate where everyone knows him. And he must mean to stay a long time if he is going to grow a yew hedge round the scented herbs and the lilies. A bit awkward about the reference to Oscar Wilde in *The Narrow Street*[152] – I wonder what it was. I hadn't read it.

I'm near to going to sleep at my post. Am chewing Horlick tablets. The wind howls and the bad influence snores. Ralph [Partridge] thinks the war will end in August.

You must be having a ghastly week without Jimmy.

The MacNeils (Fighting Cocks) were the only people I've yet heard talk against the Beveridge Plan. Joan talked in a sort of Father Orchard[153] way about it.

I must stop because when I think what to say next I go into a muse and nearly to sleep. I'll try *War and Peace*. I feel very re-stimulated over it – as Ralph on Sunday said, it is the greatest book and he often rereads it.

All love,

H

From ANNE   At home, tea time (am working at home today)
Darling Heywood,
    Have had a success with Yvonne[154] over my Mme Tussaud items

---

151 Sir Paul Latham had lately been in prison for six months.
152 A book Heywood had sent him when he was in prison.
153 That is, very Conservative.
154 Yvonne ffrench, author of a biography, *Mrs Siddons* (1954), and of numerous children's books.

– she is very pleased. She may use the sketch in her book – if I can trace its history, which I don't expect Seligman[155] will be able to do.

Have got so excruciatingly bored over paying the bills today (mostly the little men) that I have almost ceased to be able to do it. Nancy *has* ceased – it was really always *her* job (paying the little men) but she didn't protest at all when she saw me doing it yesterday. But on thinking it over I realise it's quite fair really, as she does a lot of things now she used not to do before, like the ordering. I don't see how Mollie can ever have time to do the paying as well as the sending of bills so I shall have to go on doing it for ever even on child-bed. I would far far prefer to do the sending bills to the paying ones if I could choose. At least there is the interest of seeing what people have been buying. (Grumble, grumble, grumble, grumble.)

Later, 11.30, in bed

Having Janetta and Kenneth [Sinclair-Loutit] was successful I think. It was dreadful that you weren't there though as he wanted the gramophone played. It took ages finding the needles (they were in Logan Pearsall Smith's box). I think – I hope – it was all right. I thought they were perhaps relieved to have a distraction (Jan's funeral was this morning).

I must go to sleep, I've looked up trains and will try to catch one at 9, which goes straight there, and if I miss it there's another at 9.30 which means changing at Basingstoke – both quite safe for lunch if there are buses all right.

Love from

ANNE

PS Thursday, in shop. Lovely long letter from you, which I long to answer in detail now but mustn't because of all the things to do. Mr Baer[156] is in the shop going round belittling things. He says Heffers sells your Stubbs at 21/- – sickening, isn't it?[157]

Paul Latham's letter *very* fascinating. Haven't got a *The Narrow Street* so can't look up about O. Wilde.

155 Kurt Seligman ran an art gallery in New York and later one in Paris.
156 Mr Baer ran an art gallery in Duke Street, St James's.
157 Stubbs's *Anatomy of the Horse*, reprinted by Heywood Hill in 1938. It would now sell for about £100.

Now Mr Baer has gone and Mr De Beer is here – Did *you* know they were two people? I always thought they were one.

Love
ANNE

From HEYWOOD   Larkhill

[probably Wednesday, 17 February]

Darling Anne,

For no particular reason I'm in rather a deep gloom. Everything seems particularly vile. The ghastly useless huge effort mental and physical to no good, where I'm wasting my time and your time and their time. The utter drab horror of it. And the constant humiliation of being worse than the others at everything, and not being able to be facetious about it either, but just sunk in a dumb misery, so that when someone does try to talk to me it's no good and I imagine myself – with no reason and part-indulgently – a sort of pariah. I get so sick of all their endless small-talk and cracks, and having to keep trying to laugh. I'm tired after the telephone which is why I'm in such a bad state today.

Thursday, 18th

Your three letters all arrived at once this morning. I long for Sat. Don't wait for me for lunch if I'm not there by 1.15.

What a dreadful moan this is. Don't tell people. I'll have to stop or I shan't be able to post this.

I'll answer all shop questions at weekend. Very little hope of night pass but I haven't quite given up. What's rather awful is it generally means making someone who doesn't go do more. It's strange that you had the same sort of feeling about Jan as I did. I dreamed last night that she wasn't dead, and then she turned into my grandmother.

Love – darling
H

Anne did get to Amesbury for that weekend – 20 to 22 February, and Heywood got a night pass too. Anne remembers that the trains were particularly full and slow (and very cold) owing to unexplained troop movements.

[107]

Darling H,

Things are mediocre at the shop. Feeling rather inefficient. Long to do all the things I should have done ages ago like seeing to Haldamulla[158] and Staak,[159] but as usual keep being prevented – they both take so very long.

Mrs Kentall is the one bright spot. Surpasses all our wildest expectations: Smith's residue (he never came Saturday) of about 20 books have all been packed, posted or delivered in about a couple of hours. *All* tables dusted *before* I arrived this morning. Things we had put out yesterday at 5 o'clock to be done today were packed after she got back from the post last night. And she's always coming up to me smiling and saying, 'Is there anything I can do, Madam?'

Nancy is being rather difficult, and I fear a bit bored and irritated by me, and by everything. I too have felt irritated and also indignant.[160]

Willie[161] came in and said he's in exactly the same position as you in being expected to do maths and not being able to. But he is very contemptuous of mathematical people, and thinks he and you are much better than them, so you must try very hard to feel the same. *Copy* him.

Later, still in shop

God I left this letter in the lav, where Nancy's just been – with the bit about her upward. Half covered by a Penguin, though, and she

---

158 Library of the Haldamulla (tea planters) Club in Ceylon (Sri Lanka), formerly run by Anne's tea-planter great-uncle Gilbert Hunter Blair, who had died a year of two earlier.

159 An American bookshop, a good customer.

160 James Lees-Milne records in *Ancestral Voices*: '27 February Went to tea with Anne Hill in Little Venice. She is truly one of the world's worthwhile women, so intelligent, male-minded, and deliciously humorous. I tackled her about their underpaying Nancy, which she admitted. She did not resent my interference but explained laughingly that whereas Nancy got paid £3/ 10/-, she only got £2/ 10/-; that the shop barely paid its way.'

161 William Augustus Henry King, married to Viva, had worked at the British Museum since 1914. He ended as assistant keeper in the Department of British and Medieval Antiquities. He was a convivial figure who spent much time in the Garrick Club.

said once she's not a reader (of other people's letters I mean, like I am). Let's pray that all is well. I feel very anxious.

The story of J. Maclaren-Ross in the Penguin[162] is about Maidstone I'm practically sure. As I'm practically sure the Lambes know him (isn't he on the BBC?), and said he'd once had pneumonia at Maidstone.

Fondest love from

ANNE

From HEYWOOD   Larkhill
[1st page missing]

I long to get out of this place – which strangles me. It's always agony to leave you but the weekend has made me better. I've shuffled through today without any violent exposures – except not shouting and moving loud and quick enough at the gun drill.

I've just done a maddening thing. Mummy sent me a box of acid drops and in it were letters from her and Daddy. I put the letters in my pocket to read them here in the reading room, and to tell you what D. said. They must have fallen out. They're nowhere. They weren't in an envelope – so there's no hope.

I can't make myself read up for this exam. It bores me so, and I can't understand, and there's only the old parson I could ask, and he's so busy cramming away I don't like to disturb. I'll just have to sink and hope there'll be no result.

Fondest love

HEYWOOD

To Heywood from his sister, SHEILA HILL   Shiplake Grange

Henley-on-Thames
[undated]

It was lovely to get your letter. They do so tell me everything I want to know. It is awful that all the things one really feared are there. It is never true what some psychologists say, that the actual ex-perience dispels the fears. The trapped feeling is so ghastly.

John and I stayed Friday night at the Savoy. We had a wonderful

---

162 That Anne had just sent him.

bedroom, and the echoing courtyard with deep dustbin noises out-side, and a steaming bathroom with the lavatory telephone, were just as described in some novel. – I can't remember who by. But it was very nice, like being in Paris for a moment.

John despised his new CO. He sent an aeroplane to fetch his dog from Lossiemouth (a lovely story for Daddy), but he is a deadly man and makes everyone miserable.

Can you ever read, are there any chances?

I think your attitude to it all is very high standard, yourself untouched though everything is so smashed to pieces. I think if only we can get through we shall feel everything that is nice more strongly. But your life is so much grimmer than most.

From HEYWOOD   Larkhill
                                                    Tuesday, 23 February
Darling Anne,

I didn't think there was any chance of a letter today so it was extra nice to get one.

Did Daddy write and tell you about the £25 quarterly (when he first said it, I mean) or did he only tell me?

Another dingy day is over, but not *too* awful. It's lucky it wasn't this weekend you were coming, as I have got to do the telephone job all of Sunday.

We had poached egg for tea today.

I shall have to play football on Thursday, as a lot of the old-boy specialists have been posted.

I don't think buy the Rowlandson. His books are so terribly tricky. But if you have – it doesn't matter. I was in two minds.

Don't go working too late.

                                                               Love
                                                                 H

From ANNE   10 Warwick Avenue
                        Wednesday, 24 February, evening after supper
Darling Heywood,

Tonight I spoke to Mrs Sternson about a nanny – she gave a start. She's angelic as usual – quite prepared for me to have none. She's obviously so good about babies (and for one important thing is in the habit of going to Welfare Clinics weekly) that I feel it wouldn't matter having an inexperienced if intelligent and nice person to look after the baby, *under* her. She's prepared for anything.

I'm enclosing a copy of the typescript *Ballade* by Beerbohm that was in the lot from Hodgson's February sale (we've only just got it because 2 lots got left behind by accident, or Smith's carelessness). It's rather amusing, isn't it? It's signed by him. Now what shall we charge? Please darling decide like an angel as Nancy and I *can't*. The whole lot, the poem and 5 rather shabby vols. Cost £2. 6/-. Can't remember what except *Zuleika Dobson*, but not illustrated.

Nancy and I were very excited about the poem at first, and thought of quoting it to Osbert at £5; then we were a little dashed by Propert (or Prescott? rather nice amusing intellectual very hook-nosed old queen; what *is* his name?)[163] whom we showed it to, knowing it all already and having known it since about 1912 (30 years); which I suppose, if one had thought for a moment, one might have guessed would be the case. On the other hand, the version he knew was rather different, and this being signed must be the true authentic one. So what shall we charge for it?

The 12 vol. Gibbon, also from the Jan. lot, is *extremely* nice, beautiful green mottled calf in very good condition, with nice illustrations. In the same lot was Plutarch's *Lives*, 6 vols., calf, 1813, nothing very wonderful but quite all right (a bit rubbed and rough; will give it to Mrs K. to polish). The lot for £3. 12/6. We provisionally marked the Gibbon £8, the Plutarch £2. 10/-. Do you think that's all right?

The Reresby Travels is *lovely* too – cost £4. 10/-, we've marked it £10. Haven't had time to look at the rest of the Feb. lot yet.

The annoying thing about both the books from Beach[164] and about the last Hodgson lot of things, was that Nancy unpacked them and placed them all here and there, after marking them all herself, without my ever having seen them, while I was at home one day. I was very cross about this, as it's quite maddening and means I don't know where any of them are of course. And since you've been gone I've always priced the new old books (which I do usually consult Nancy about, as she's rather good at it). I suppose I also minded because opening the parcels when one knows there are

163 Prescott was his name.
164 D. M. Beach, a well-established bookshop in Salisbury.

exciting things in them is one of the most enjoyable things of all in the shop, and then the being able to look at them really properly, at leisure, and for the pleasure as well as for the pricing.

Anyhow, now I'm going to take the Beach receipt and the Hodgson invoices and find them all, even though it'll waste a lot of time. I *must* know where they all are. I think I'll have to 'say something' to N. Rather difficult to know what and how, without seeming bossy and touchy. Quite easy if one's in exactly the right frame of mind, but easy to blunder if not.

I don't think Nancy can have read my letter (the one I left in the lavatory), or if she has she's taken up some very wonderful attitude towards it. I hope she hasn't, as it said much more and worse things than I really feel about her. The criticism I have to make is that she does not remember much that it is our shop; also she's Smithish about things she doesn't like doing. But I do enjoy her company in the shop for a great proportion of the time, very much. Also I find her invaluable in helping me make a decision about Merino buying, whether something is nice or not, and how much to charge, even if I sometimes disagree with her. The great thing is, she is fundamentally extremely congenial, which is an extraordinary piece of luck, when you think of what sort of ghastly person might be working here now. And it must be irritating for her often not doing what she'd like to do, and having to do things that bore her. It is those sort of stresses of shop life that cause the difficulties there are. It would be less so if you were in the shop and not me, as you really know far far *far* more than her, and me only a bit more.

Three days later

Mrs Kentall is beyond belief wonderful. Really the change from the Smiths to her is like being raised from hell to heaven. I should think it is almost literally true that the Smiths must be almost the worst workers in London (Jimmy I should say quite the worst), and her quite the best. She posts the letters all day so that people get letters we write in the morning in the evening.[165] And everything is posted or delivered the day we put it on the table. She is always nipping to Belgrave Square and back again and then to Grosvenor Square and Cumberland Court, several times a day, and taking about 5 minutes each time. Expeditions that with the Smiths loomed like going to

165 An astonishing testament to the post in the war, especially compared with what happens now.

the Arctic (and were put off for days and days). I long to make them know (though I won't). Today I gave her the invoices to enter in her spare time, expecting her to take about a week as she has such a lot to do (Jimmy would have taken 2 or 3 months), and she came back with them all beautifully neatly done in about an hour (it takes Nancy or me quite 3 or 4). She's already this morning, alone, dusted, taking each book out, the *whole* of Big White – I must admit rearranging it very confusingly and unfindably, all the books in order of height.

But one thing I fear sadly is certain – we shall *never* be allowed to keep Nancy and Mollie and Mrs K, and quite possibly I should think two might be taken – I forget if I told you I've already had a form only allowing Nancy to stay till August (though Nancy being 38 and delicate I'm pretty sure of renewing that I think). I fear Mrs K is particularly precarious, as she has some agricultural stamps on her insurance card, which is a very bad thing to have, it appears. And I can't make everyone out to be key, though God knows they all are. I believe they are getting appallingly strict, quick, thorough and sudden about calling up now.[166]

Thursday

Working at home today. How *dreadful* you having to play football – today it will be, very soon I should think (it's not 10 past 1). Also, the exams must be a nightmare. I long to hear all about both.

The next time I come and stay I think I shall come on Friday in spite of the expense (the Avon was £4. 18. 6), as last week it was too short I thought. Only Saturday did I fully enjoy myself, as all Sunday nearly I felt depressed about leaving. I think partly it was the weather.

Fondest, devoted love from
ANNE

From HEYWOOD   Larkhill
                                              Wednesday 24 February

Darling Anne,
    It is the one bright spot about Mrs K. It's a miracle she's there. I

166 That is to say, Anne expected that one or even two of the people helping her in the shop – Nancy Mitford, Mollie Frieze-Green and the new and wonderful Mrs Kentall – might be called to some form of war work.

should try awfully hard to give her something to do *in* the shop sometimes. Regular times as far as poss. because then it won't be vague and moulder to nothing. It would probably make her more interested and feel appreciated. Though I know that there will always seem too much to do downstairs. How awful about the letter and Nancy – I don't expect she read it on that paper, it looks too unletterish. Anyhow you'll probably know by now.

I shan't be able to do anything or write properly till this exam is over which assumes fantastic nonsensical proportions. Everyone's talking about it so much. The awful thing is that I know I give the impression of not trying, whereas it is really self-conscious clumsiness, dumbness and knotted tangle. The old parson is the only one who does help me a bit but I can't really take it in. There are so many subjects all nearly the same. I sucked up to the old parson by asking to look at the polyfoto[167] of his daughter, and gazing for hours at it, and saying which I thought were the best. She looked surprisingly pretty, as he's such an old crab. He's North Country, and says, 'I must go to the lavatory.' About the others – I've developed an intense dislike of the Charterhouse man, though he's amiable. He's always shouting out facetious drill commands, and making tiresome jokes, and showing off in the most deadly way. I need a foreigner or freak to make friends with. They're all dead normal. Decent chaps.

I must stop now and gaze at my notebook. The parson is on telephones tonight. I shall probably not write at all tomorrow. I end by gazing at the contemporary lithographs. I wouldn't like to have one at home. They're too flat and poster-like. It as a marvellous warm spring sort of day today – it made me long to run right away, and to imagine myself on every bus that went by. I hope Mama is coming to you for the weekend.

Love – darling Anne

HEYWOOD

Thanks for Penguin. It'll be a nice treat for after the exams. I'll be able to read it on the telephones on Sunday. I'm on them from 8 a.m. to 6 p.m., but I don't mind very much. I shall go to Fighting Cocks for a bath on Sat.

---

167 The system, common with photographers then, particularly with portraits, of sending a sheet with numerous small versions from which one or two could be chosen to have blown up.

From ANNE   10 Warwick Avenue
                                             Thursday, 25.2.43
Darling H,
   Have been having a very boring day at home doing shop accounts. Only been out for 10 minutes to post your letter, drop the
remains of Smith wages in their letterbox, and walk once round the
canal junction. I meant to go for a proper hour's walk, but put it off
so long that it rained.

                                             Later after dinner
The Devases[168] have rung up and I've said I'll have dinner with
them on Wed. Though I like them, I now feel rather appalled at the
thought of the effort. Also, possibly Ma may be here and I shall
have to put them off. Awkwardness.

                                             Friday 26th
Today is your dreadful exam day. I do think it's awful for you; at
least by the time you get this it will be over.
   A glorious wonderful day, that makes me long for normal life.
The cabbages are all alive and green, though absolutely tiny. There
is an incredible amount of green leaf in the garden, exactly like the
beginning of April. The forsythia is about 2 months early, struggling in a pathetic weak way; there will be a few yellow buds on it I
think in about a fortnight. I might post them to you.
   I must stop writing and work. Sheila is coming to lunch which
will be nice. She's on her way to Stradishall[169] for the weekend.
Will post this early so that you are sure to get it Sat.
                                 Much love darling from
                                             ANNE

From HEYWOOD   Larkhill
                                             Friday, 26 February
Darling Anne,
   The exam is over. I've done just as badly as I thought I would and
am certain to be bottom and to have failed – but it's a great relief it's
over and not to feel I must read notebooks all night. I suppose now

168 Anthony and Nicolette Devas. See *Two Flamboyant Fathers* by Nicolette Devas,
1966.
169 Where John Hill was stationed.

[115]

I'll be seen by the Major – and if a transfer doesn't come through, I may be sent to an ordinary gunner squad. That of course would be dreadful, and I'd have to do gun drill all day, every day.

Today began badly with the bombardier pulling my blankets off and shouting 'Get up' and then 'Here's a fellow who sleeps with a scarf on.' (Lucky I didn't bring father's balaclava.) He's not bad really, the bombardier – a weak embittered man – who has to do things like that to seem hearty. He shouts 'Rise and shine!' at 6 o'clock in the morning and then goes round pulling men's blankets off. Then I had to queue for the wash basin and missed my turn by someone else shoving in. And some kindly person said, 'And how's Mr Hill this morning?' Whatever does one answer? I'm amazed at the answers people always have ready to everything.

I'm getting quite good at climbing the rope upside down. There's a new way he's starting to make us do it – to crawl up a slanting rope – which I think will be impossible.

I nearly exploded with strain and confusion during the exam. The old parson has obviously done well because he's perky and pleased with himself. I'm writing this in the barrack room – boldly sitting at the table in the middle of the room. A game of draughts is going on at my elbow, and men are peering over at a great talking group on the other side. And the wireless of course. Great looking-over dangers. There's always a danger or dread. I did rather well with chocolate in the NAAFI this week. Got 4 threepenny blocks.

The Sunday Times Reading Room has shut for a fortnight for an art exhibition – which is another bore.

I'm sure you're right about an inexperienced Nanny under Mrs S. being all right. Had she any ideas about what you could do? How about a gas ring in the bedroom? I think I'll answer shop questions when I'm doing telephones on Sunday and send this tomorrow – so that you'll get it on Monday. I can't think how you can go on carrying that great weight of Harriet about with you. You do it so wonderfully. It must be so hampering and exhausting.

This week has been a fairly dreadful one, and I've felt wretched, but I felt much better tonight, and quite friendly again towards the Charterhouse man. Probably because he's done badly too in the exam. Isn't it all extraordinarily exactly like school – but without the hols to look forward to. I shall be awfully crabbed and warped and irritable when I do get back. It forces me to think endlessly about myself.

How very annoying about Nancy and the Hodgson books. I suppose she couldn't be bribed to leave all the marking of old books to you by giving all the ordering of new ones to her?

You *will* have days off now won't you? I can see Nancy is just like I was at Sawyers. Kicking against the pricks. Did Craig Macfarlane answer?[170]

All my love

H

From ANNE
10 Warwick Avenue

27 February – Sat. 9 o'clock

Darling Heywood,

Feeling rather drained of mental energy after reading about 50 pages of the *Clique* without stopping (not to much effect).

I wonder how the exam went. I do hope not too ghastly and horrible. It is very sad that you will have to be indoors doing telephones all tomorrow, if it is such a lovely day as this again. I really did walk a lot today. Coming back from the shop got out half way up Edgware Road and went in and out of Church Street, and the various streets parallel to it, looking at the shops and stalls. Bought a *Jane Eyre* and *John Inglesant* (both in good condition) for 1/- each. Otherwise there wasn't anything much. Jim [Lees-Milne] came to tea and I walked back with him to Hyde Park Corner, then back to Marble Arch. I'd meant to have dinner at Lyons (at 6.30) but there was a queue all along Oxford Street. So I went I fear to the Great Western at Paddington (where one can't pay less than 5/- now). One rather worrying thing – Midi Gascoigne has told Jim that Nancy told her she didn't know if she could go on living on the wages we give her, as that was practically all she had to live on. Midi told Jim to tell me this. She also said that Nancy did like the shop very much. I have had an idea that she might be discontented with her wages for some time. I think she should have more, don't you? Do you think 10/-? Or £1? Please say what you think. I suppose I shall have to cut my wages. An annoying thing now is having to pay the Lesters, when Mrs K. would do what they do in about 10 minutes each morning – she's quite six times faster than they are. But I daren't ask them to leave. Though they'd certainly find work

170 Solicitor to Heywood and Anne and to the bookshop. Also a personal friend.

without the slightest difficulty if we did. As that's so, perhaps I'd better sound them.

What do you feel when I write endlessly about the shop as I fear I do? Endlessly and boringly. I get bored myself.

However, I will go on a moment or two longer and say: I've been doing better by Malcolm again lately. A good deal thanks to Mrs K., and of course luck, one or two things he's wanted he's had very quickly. I've evolved a system now, of when the Stationery Office sends us samples of those 'Front Line' type of things (which they do all the time) I at *once* forward them to Malcolm telling him if he wants them he must let me know by Tuesday (say) (he generally orders 50). Also, I've got the Hodder traveller to promise to send me 3 each of all 2/6 Westerns as they are published and come into stock, and six each of the Wright and Brown ones that are under 4/6. It is very tantalising, as Malcolm has £50 to spend on Westerns but I doubt if we'll be able to get anything like as many as that. I'm going to put an *advertisement* in the *Clique* for them as well.

Sunday, 12.30, in bed

I've been writing to Staak this morning comfortably in bed; one great heavy weight off my chest. And Haldamulla went last week, so feel am gradually catching up. I wonder how you're getting on at the telephone. It is dreadful how much worse your life is than mine. I sometimes almost wish I could be an AT[171] (but not quite). As I sit in the evenings comfortably in front of the fire, having my food brought up to me, I constantly and painfully think of you, alone in the dreary Sunday Times Reading Room, or worse beneath the blaring loud speaker with all those people.

Love darling Heywood

ANNE

Later

Where's *The Anatomy of Bibliomania*? Someone *urgently immediately* wants it. No other particular news. I'll post this now to get to you Monday. Tonight Coney is coming to dinner, at Norway so that the Sternsons can have a rest (Mrs S. has a cold). Monday I'll go out somewhere as it's his night off. I was in all last week. Wednesday the Devases.

171 That is, join the Army. The ATS – Auxiliary Territorial Service – was later superseded by the WRACS – the Women's Royal Army Corps.

Don't force yourself to write ever day if it's very difficult with the course. I think it's promising that far more people passed the last course than the one before, as it may mean they want people so badly they are lowering their standards and making it easier.

From HEYWOOD   Larkhill
                                              Sunday, 28 February
Darling Anne,

I had to get up in a scramble this morning – they didn't turn the lights on till 10 minutes before breakfast and I had to be here in half an hour, and so I've left your letter with the shop questions behind. I'll try to remember them.

I've just been sent on an errand to find Sergeant White to tell him that 'they' are sending 30 men on church parade. Who 'they' were I couldn't make out. I went to the hut where Sergeant White sleeps and wandered round asking where Sergeant White was. He wasn't there. He might be in the 2nd brick block. I went to the 2nd brick block where they were throwing 'biscuits' (the 3 separate stuffed pads which make up one's mattress) out of the windows because the ATS are moving in there. I was nearly hit by a biscuit, and wandered round asking for White, but White wasn't there either, so I came back here. They think he must have paraded on Battery Square, while the others were parading on Regimental Square, because of some confusion in some order. Almost every errand one goes on is similarly Kafka-like.

Yesterday morning in class they went over the exam paper and I was appalled at the mistakes I must have made. In the last half hour before lunch they had a discussion on education. Everyone agreed that the public schools should be opened to all, and the school age raised in all schools run by the state. I'd rather have liked to try to say something, but never gathered myself up together in time. Then they went on about a universal language – whether there should or would be one. Most said shouldn't or wouldn't.

After lunch there was a parade of the whole battery because a man had lost a rifle. That annoyed everyone very much because there never is a parade on Sat. afternoon. It took an hour while they looked at all our rifles and searched in our barrack rooms while we weren't there. In the end they found the rifle in the battery store, because a man going on leave had mistakenly taken another man's and left it in the stores, and the other man had taken his. I had a fear they might find it under my bed, which would have brought down the fury of hundreds.

After that I walked down to Amesbury. I enjoyed that – being away and alone – as soon as I left the huts and the country began. The food is very good at the MacNeils. Cakes and scones for tea – fish and duck for dinner. A bath in between, and they go into the garden and leave me alone. If ever a copy of *War and Peace* does turn up I'd like to give it her to repay a bit. She's appallingly conservative and die-hard, and almost fanatical about everything. Anti-Jew, anti altering schools, anti-Russia. I put in a few little feeble wedges. One can't help liking her despite her atrocious views.

Perhaps – do you think – if sales of old books are not good at the shop we ought to go slow in buying? – or else we'll get too badly overdrawn. I don't know. Maybe it's better to have the stock, which we could resell in a sale if we sink (don't particularly bother to answer this). I think it's important to try to train Mrs K. a bit to the shop – as there are bound to be long time gaps to fill when you're away.

It's stuffy in this small room and I'm becoming bemused.

That Max Beerbohm lot was cheap. Was it a 1st edit. of *Zuleika Dobson*? Do look (it might have said in the catalogue). I don't think the 1st edit. was illustrated. I should think £5 for the typescript poem all right if we can somehow prove it to be original. Perhaps someone like Osbert might even ask Max. Those prices for Gibbon and Plutarch sound all right. Possibly £7. 10/- for Gibbon and £3. 10/- for Plutarch.

It's amusing the Max being about George V. I do enjoy *War and Peace* very much. The further it gets the wiser it seems. And all that he says about war seems good. He makes the characters visible and true. And bits about Napoleon are interesting.

Did you try for *Teach Yourself German*? Bound to be imposs. If we have to go on being something I think we must try to go on being booksellers. All this hideous life here and seeing the others and listening to the talk about their own dull lives makes me know how much better our job is for ourselves. How I long for our life together again. How more and more I think the Partridges are right. Some gloomy soldier discussing the war in here with the other said he thought it would go on till 1948.

I'm going to try to dash down to the Avon tonight and meet

Derek [Hill] – but after 6 I'm supposed to be laying a fire in the locker room with the old parson and finding bits of wood from nowhere.

If my vest is washed by the end of the week, could you send it me and I'll send you a dirty one.

I meant to send you a long nice letter today but this is very deadly.

Look after yourself – my dear – and fight against shop frets and bear up. I've managed to write to Father. Now there's old Malcolm.

True love from
HEYWOOD

From HEYWOOD   Larkhill
Monday, 1 March

Darling,

It's splendid – isn't it, getting the 48 hours? Two are now allowed to go each weekend and the sergeant said who wants one? And I held up my hand and got it – (though did in some other wretch). I hope it doesn't mean lots of complications for you – Mama and all. We're not supposed to leave till 4 so I shouldn't get to you till about 8 on Friday. I suppose if the posting does happen to come before it will then all be off. We might go to *A Month in the Country*, either Sat. afternoon or evening? Derek [Hill] says it's good. If you'd like to – will you get seats? I wouldn't mind going to the shop Sat morning. Whatever you want. Would quite like to – but you might hate it. I have to catch a train back at 7 o'clock Sunday evening – so that's not too bad. I'd quite like to see Lambes or Griffins or Malcolm, or anyone nice, but don't bother to particularly arrange. I won't talk about it too much in case it doesn't happen.

I had dinner with Derek at the Avon last night. He'd spent the day going to see Nic and Jonny at Port Regis.[172] He said they were in terrific form. Very well and completely uncowed, and tore him over the school pointing out this and that, and shouting things like 'That's the head boy!' It all sounded too good to be true.

I've been down to the call box, but there was a long queue, so went back and had supper. It looks as if I won't manage it tonight. I'm now in the Salvation Army hut because it's near the box. I've

172 Nic Hill and Jonny Gathorne-Hardy (see Appendix). Port Regis was their prep school.

never been there before. It's the same as all the others – crowded and village-hallish with hideously painted boards.

No exam results yet – but I'm not worrying nearly so much about it now. We spent the afternoon in a shed firing pellets out of a howitzer at a moving cardboard tank. Everyone had to shout commands as well. 'Target, tank, half left, 500 yards', and then move the gun about. Nobody heard me of course.

I shan't be able to write much. Am going to the Aunts to dinner tomorrow. Telephones again on Wed. night. Route march and football Thurs. – so what with the little sleep will be semiconscious.

Love
H

4

Wentworth Woodhouse

From HEYWOOD   14335674 Gnr. G. H. Hill

No 2 Coy IC Depot

That's enough address.   Nr Rotherham

I'm still Gnr.   Yorkshire

Monday, 8 March

Darling,

I got here about 7. Lots of muddling trains and buses from Sheffield. On the edge of a huge park belonging to Lord Fitzwilliam. I'm
in an awful state of not knowing what to do and wear. Nobody
arrived with me, and I'm a week after the last intake, and they seem
to know nothing about me. I was marched before a Guards officer
who was baffled. I've been joined to a squad, but as they've been
doing it all for a week it's very confusing, and I'm not in the same
room as there are no beds – but in a sort of small room for strays,
so I never know what to put on. I gather it's all v. strict. Back to
blanco and polish and drill and rifles and Bren guns and unarmed
combat. No special course about photos or anything, so perhaps
I'm still in the wrong place. I'll have to spend all the week getting things clean and blancoed, so shan't be able to write much.
Can't find a phone or post office or anything. It's all in the huge
stone stables of the big house. Pretty on the outside. Washing and
lavatories very poor.

The extraordinary thing is that Albert[173] is here. I don't feel
somehow as pleased as I might. He's been here four weeks. Only
saw him for a moment in the NAAFI but am seeing him this evening, when I hope he'll tell me things.

Wentworth Woodhouse

Tuesday, 9 March

I've just been told I am to see the training officer tomorrow at ¼ to

173 Albert was an old friend of Heywood.

[123]

9 – so maybe I'll be told something definite then. I don't think I'll ever get through any of these courses unless they're more interesting than they've been so far, and then all the circumstances are so paralysing.

Here I am dirging on again just as I said I would. I feel forlorn and such miles away from you. I'm afraid that it's too long and difficult and complicated for you to come to, and that you ought not.

There's no noticeable distinction of age, or class. Today I've had a few words with Albert, but not with the others yet. I attended a lecture on map reading – a lecture on the organisation of a division, a religious discussion (very odd that, in an attic with a plain clothes parson. An ex-Sunday school teacher did most of the talking.) Then rifle drill; then pistol drill. I think the interview will get me off the route march.

It was so lovely being at home with you.

H

From HEYWOOD   Wentworth Woodhouse
                                    Wednesday, 10 March 1943
Darling Anne,

I was seen for a second by the training officer this morning. They had altered the time but hadn't told me and he was in a great rush. 'You're an earmarked man, aren't you?' he said. I said, 'Yes, sir.' He asked me how long I'd been in, if I'd done a firing course (I have) and if I'd had any leave. So it's just *faintly* possible I might get some leave. I wouldn't mention it except to prepare you for the faint possibility. He didn't say any more except 'All right.' He was in a great hurry and fluster. Anyhow it got me off this morning's route march. I've spent the morning putting bundles of dirty washing into sacks. This afternoon I've got to load the sacks on to a lorry and maybe go to Sheffield to unload them. Could you send me a smallish quantity of lavatory paper. The lavs are primitive – earth and exposed to all. I long to walk in the park which looks lovely – and so is the weather. Perhaps I'll be able to on Saturday.

I had a ten-minute talk with Albert last night. He's been here 4 weeks and is now working very hard at an exam. He's taken a room in the village with three others – where he works. If I stay here I shall have to try to find one, as there's no escape room, and the NAAFI is wretched as always.

The motor biking here sounds terrifying. Up cliffs and through rivers. 3 weeks of it.

There are only two other men sleeping in my room – other strays, quite amiable – both been in a long time and hardened. The room is used by sergeants and people in the day time.

All my love

H

From HEYWOOD   Wentworth Woodhouse
                                      Wednesday, 10 March

Darling Anne,

I had to cut off this morning's letter to get it posted. I went on with the washing this afternoon. With a Scottish youth I had to load the bundles into a van, and then lie on the bundles in the back, and drive into the laundry in Sheffield and unload them. The Scottish youth made whistling noises at girls on the way, I found it very difficult to understand what he said, but I rather enjoyed it. It was strange inside the laundry, thousands of girls in cubicles and the Assommoir[174] smell, and then we went upstairs and were given a cup of tea. On the way back the driver illegally stopped at some public baths, and we had a quick bath. I was given some bundles of clean washing to give to a store-keeper here but the store-keeper of course wasn't there, so I've still got them, and shall have them all night. I can't make out whether I have to do the course here before I do a photo course. The next course here doesn't start for two weeks, and meanwhile I'm vaguely attached to the course now in progress, though it's no good beginning in the middle. If nothing happens in the next day or two, I think I'll try to ask if I can have some leave. I don't want to ask at once in case the officer I saw this morning is doing something. It's a bore that he was in a rush.

I hope they won't move me out of the room I'm in, where I'm alone quite a lot, and tonight there's a fire. It's very like the top room in a stable – which it is. Great thick whitewashed walls and a wood floor and low windows to the floor. There's a melancholy corporal in it now. I've tried to ask him questions about things, but he's too sunk in his gloom. There's also a noisy tricky man, but he's out most of the time, and comes in late at night. I believe I'm

---

174 Assommoir smell. A reference to the novel *L'Assommoir* by Zola (1877).

to spend all tomorrow cleaning the room – which won't be bad. Could you send me some pants. I haven't been able to get out at all yet, but shall over the weekend – to the village. Rotherham is a hideous suburb of Sheffield.

All the people on the journey were astoundingly kind. A woman in the train insisted on paying my fare. The girl at the station buffet gave me tea. A man in another train said call on his family. A pub-keeper gave me huge tea and wouldn't let me pay. A shop woman let me buy chocolate.

All my love

H

Many letters went astray while Heywood was at Wentworth Woodhouse. There are none from Anne for the first three weeks, and none from Heywood between the 10th and 20th of March.

He had home leave from Wednesday 17th to Friday 19 March.

From ANNE   10 Warwick Avenue
                                            Saturday, 20 March 1943

Darling Heywood,

Got your telegram about ¼ to 6. Too late to send the £1 in time to get you Monday I fear. Will though tomorrow.

Have felt melancholy and anxious all day today. At the shop felt saddened and worried by the sense of it all passing from my control, and I don't like the not ordering new books myself. When I said to Nancy (I thought flatteringly and it was intended to please her) '*You'd* better have this *Times Literary Supplement* over the weekend instead of me, as you're ordering now,' she said, 'Well, I shan't look at it till next week', ungraciously. I suppose thinking I was trying to make her work at weekends too or something. It's going to be so difficult and agonising reading reviews and not ordering, and feeling bound and un-independent.[175]

Mollie has asked to do the paying of the bills now. That I am pleased about, except I can't think how she can possibly have time in only 3½ days a week. The thing is that you and I really (including clique-reading etc. over weekends) worked at least six

175 Anne was to leave the shop on 16 April to go and have the baby at Ronans, the Lambes' house.

whole long days a week normally – through a sort of inefficiency, untidiness and I don't know what quite – procrastination and day-dreaming.

I slightly dread the endless complicated explaining that will have to be gone through before she will be able to do it. But she is exceptionally quick and intelligent at understanding and remembering that sort of thing.

Today I have longed intensely and continuously for you to come home permanently. I keep finding myself thinking and racking my brains about it, as if, if I could only think *hard* enough, I could think of a way by which you *could*. The same feeling as I have about children's names, that round the corner, if only one could remember it, is a better name than any we've ever thought of.

Last night Ruth, Fidelity and I went out to an Edgware Road cinema (Bing Crosby) then had dinner at the Great Western. I thought that at that very time you must be so miserable arriving back, all alone and beset by worries and fears.

Sunday

I'm so sorry but can only send 10/- today. I've no more and neither have the Sternsons, and I can't think of anyone to borrow from. I'll send you another 10/- tomorrow.

Have written to Wesson, not a very good letter. Am now going to the post, and if I can bear the boredom for ½ an hour's walk.[176]

Fond devoted love

ANNE

From HEYWOOD   Wentworth Woodhouse
                                                  Saturday, 20 March

Darling,

The taxi was waiting and I got to the stables soon after 9. I wasn't allowed to stay in my nice room, but was shoved into a huge ordinary one, and was just able to get settled on the only spare bunk – a high top one – before lights out. This morning I was told first to sweep the courtyard. Great difficulty in getting a broom and then the head kept falling off, and the sergeant kept shouting I wasn't to idle. Then joined to a squad and drilled for 2 hours. Then

176 The doctor had told Anne she should have daily walks, the longer the better.

change into PT things and a run through the park – not too bad, then ½ hour peeling potatoes. Then lunch. I went into the village. It's small, and only 1 or 2 very villagey shops, and the post-office was shut. Then I asked one or two cottages if they had rooms for hire, but they were all full up. One of them was extraordinary – a woman covered in bandages – man asleep on the sofa, and daughter with bare feet. Then I didn't know what to do – so stood in a queue for a bus for Rotherham and that's where I am now. I went to the YMCA to write this, but small and crowded – then to a café, where I had some fishcakes at 4 o'clock, but too crowded to write – people queuing. Now I'm in the 'best' hotel, which is drab and mournful and like a bad station hotel. They only serve meals to residents, but have allowed me to write. There's a new intake coming in on Wednesday – so maybe I'm to do the ordinary course with them.

They hadn't got your letters for me – so God knows what's happened to them. I made them look through everything. I should put Intelligence Corps Depot in full. I suppose there's still a chance I may get to Matlock, but I'd tell the letter people before.

It's ghastly of course being back again, and I feel immensely miserable, and low, and keep thinking of 'this time last week', and so on. But I think it will be better when I do definitely start on something or other, and with people who are also new. I'm now with people who are just finishing their courses and are maddeningly cheerful because they have. I feel in the the absolute depths of despair now, the grey day, and the hideous town, and hideous hotel, and the trams outside – I feel such miles away from you. But it will end I know, and it won't be frightfully long, though it does seem so now. Send a few bits more of lav. paper. I may not write much at first – there's nowhere to do it. Perhaps the NAAFI.

Fondest love – darling, darling Anne

HEYWOOD

I feel I was much too over-fussy about all the little shop and house and money things. *Only* take care of yourself and Harriet.

From HEYWOOD   Wentworth Woodhouse
                               Sunday, 21 March

Darling,

I'm feeling a bit better today. I've discovered a man who is also going to do the photos. He doesn't know any more than I do –

except that he thinks that it starts on Wednesday and not here. He doesn't know whether it's Matlock or not. He thinks they'll probably tell us tomorrow. He says it's a stiff course – which is alarming. He seems quite a nice man, but a bit frighteningly brisk and alert and competent and knowledgeable. I was in a very deep gloom when I wrote last night. I had to clean out a washhouse this morning. Scour the bowls, swab the floor, polish the taps. That was over by 11 and now there's nothing more. I am wondering whether to make a dash for Renishaw this afternoon, but can't find out about buses or exactly how far it is.

I'm short of money which is a bore, and shall probably just miss a letter if you've sent one. I'll have to keep on trying to wire or ring up. I've got about 10/– left. If I could get to Renishaw I could borrow from Osbert.

Love

H

Postcard from OSBERT SITWELL to Anne.   Renishaw
Sunday, 6.30 p.m. [21 March]
Heywood has arrived for tea and dinner, and is looking radiantly well, but very cross, and distinguished in a cross way. We miss you and wish you were here.

I am certain H. will be confined to barracks tonight, as it isn't very easy to get back.

Isn't the war *splendid*. I'm loving every minute of it.

OSBERT

From HEYWOOD   Wentworth Woodhouse
Monday, 22 March
Darling,

I think I'm off to morrow and I think to Matlock. I know I'm going, but I don't know yet for certain whether tomorrow or the day after, and I'm not sure about Matlock, but think so.

This is just to let you know. I'll write full description of Renishaw as soon as there's time. V. nice and successful and I just got back in time. I think that that same man is the only one going too. Feeling much better now. Expect more gloom as soon as the next place starts!

Haven't heard from you yet. Post feeble and slow.

Love

H

From HEYWOOD   Wentworth Woodhouse
Monday and Tuesday, 22nd and 23 March

Darling,

I'm definitely off to Matlock – early tomorrow morning. Break-fast at 7 and ready by 7.30, so it'll be a rush as always. I haven't had a chance to ring you up. Albert came to help me with equipment tonight which was touching of him, and we've just been to the pub in the village and the YMCA for supper. He's promised his girl that he'll get engaged to her this next weekend. He's been 2½ years courting. She's called Monica Hill.

Renishaw was fascinating. I'm immensely pleased I made the effort. V. tricky as I'd no idea how far or about buses or anything, and Osbert didn't really know. He bore the shock of a sudden ringing-up very well. I took a bus to Sheffield, and another from there to Eckington. I seemed to be getting miles and miles away, and wondered if I'd ever get back. The bus stopped at the park gates. It was a lovely afternoon. I walked up a hill across the park, and there was Osbert on the doorstep, in corduroy trousers, seeing some people off in a taxi. He fixed the taxi to come back for me at 9.20, so that meant a nice long time. Otherwise I'd have had to leave again at once. He apologised for Edith not being present, but said she was in bed, and would come down to dinner. That was just right.

Then he ordered more tea to be made for me. It was 5 o'clock. China or Indian? He rushed me from room to room – saying was he rushing me? – showing pictures by terrific artists. It's not quite such a huge grand house as it looks in the postcards. It's romantic and very nice. Everything is what we'd like to have in the shop if we could find and pay. (Or at Warwick Av.) Pretty wallpapers. I saw David's[177] bedroom and Osbert's bedroom. Osbert's bed had some mysterious-looking prop sticking up from under the sheets. Then he said we must go for a walk, and we went round the grounds and outhouses and down to a lake, and he was never quite sure when

177 David Horner.

we got to a place if it was really worth showing. It's high up, and you see a long way (wonderful for you that would be) to coal mines and chimneys, and the trees are black like in London.

Then a wonderful bath, all prepared and poured out with scent in it. Then the excitement of waiting for Edith to appear. No electric light – dim lamps and candles. She appeared. In a fur coat. Tall, and fatter than I thought she'd be. Fat high up. Face rather fat, and white nose, tapering more like Sachie's[178] than Osbert's. Dignified, though not too. I thought she'd be very nice. Kind, sympathetic, amusing. One would want time with her. Like O. – terrified of illness I suspect. I felt pleased and proud to be having dinner alone with them, and a little drunk; it all seemed wonderful. There was a 4-course delicious dinner. After 9 we all began to get in a fever about the taxi not coming in time, and if I'd be late.

I told them about the motto on Daddy's framed testimonial thing he'd got given when he left his company after the last war – 'Turn down the empty glass. The stars are setting and the caravan starts for the dawn of nothing.' That was a success. Edith said she'd think about it in bed.

I'm in the train now for Matlock. Change at Sheffield and Derby. Get there 12.30. Awful agitations getting off. The other man is with me. Mackenzie he's called. Rather somehow physically unpleasant, but so far amiable. I wonder if your letters will ever be forwarded.[179]

Darling, love

H

178 Sacheverell Sitwell (who had written the introduction to *Country House Baroque*).
179 They weren't, except for the one dated 20 March.

5

Smedley's Hydro, Matlock

From HEYWOOD

Gnr. G.H. Hill
PIW, Smedley's Hydro
Matlock, Derbyshire
Tuesday, 23 March

Darling Anne,

First impressions here are comparatively wonderful. It's in a huge ex-grand hotel. I'm in a room on the top floor with only 3 others in it. Separate bed and real pillow cases. There are baths and hot water and a wonderful view from the window. A sort of Rhine valley vista across the town in the valley to hills opposite, and a castle on one ... The other 3 in the room are Mackenzie – the man I came with – who I think will turn into a bore, but not offensive, and two others who seem mild and pleasant. The others are already having technical talks about lenses and things. But anyhow, it'll be five weeks much physically better. It seems incredible to be able to sit on one's bed and write, with sun pouring in. I think the course will be very intensive – so probably I won't be able to write much.

If the thinnish khaki socks that I brought back to be washed have emerged yet, – 2 pairs I think – I'd like them. Also another vest.

I long to hear how you are, and it seems ages before I can possibly get a letter from you. I do wish you could come here for a weekend. It looks as if there'll be lovely walks – but it's a long journey, and then I may have to work feverishly all the time. Tell me exactly how you are, and what Saunders said.

Love

H

From ANNE   10 Warwick Avenue
                                          Wednesday, 24 March

Darling Heywood,

I haven't gone to the Richardsons[180] after all, as someone has got
a cold. I have rather too, so am very glad.

I went to Saunders, who says the baby is in the best of the 4 main
possible positions it can be in. The position is called L.O.W. but I
can't remember what that stands for, and can only think of Left
Open White, which sounds dreadful. He said its head was nice and
get-at-able – for him, he meant – at birth, and the whole baby was
not too large (which I can hardly believe when I look at myself).
When he took my blood pressure, I thought I'd better tell him I'd
been taking Quinisan in case it made any difference, and he was
horrified and said quinine is given to people when their baby is late
to bring it on, and I must stop at *once*. However, it doesn't seem to
have done any harm. I have to go again today fortnight.

Your account of Renishaw was enthralling. You must try and get
there again. It is maddening that you are near there, and at this
beautiful romantic spa, just when I can't move (I asked Saunders
and he was too discouraging for me really to feel justified in going;
but he said if *vital* I *could*, so if you get ill or have an accident I
will).

It is wonderful that you are lying with your head on a pillow-slip
in a sunny room with this Rhineland vista. I hope today's course is
not ruining it all, and that some amiable sympathetic companion
turns up.

This is a dull letter; I have been working at home so there is no
news. I bought Rossie[181] a rather nice green wooden engine from
Coulsey[182] for 8/6, combining two necessary things, to please the
Sternsons, and to please Coulsey – (I think it also did please
Rossie). I then asked Coulsey if some nutty things in his shop were
on coupons (knowing they were), but he disappointingly just said
yes they were, without offering me them without, despite my
having been such a good customer.

I think I shall go to bed now (it's ten). Mrs S.'s sister and brother-
in-law are sleeping here tonight in the nursery.

180 Maurice and Bridget Richardson. Maurice was a gifted writer and journalist.
181 Rossie was the Sternsons' small son.
182 Stationer and sweetshop in the Harrow Road, near Warwick Avenue.

What does PIW stand for? Photographic Interpretation What? I do hope at least you got my letter sent out PIW.

Much love from
ANNE

PS Mr Merino says about the 2 books he showed you that you hesitated about, the Chippendale book at £6, and the other old book of architecture c. 1600 at £8, that now he will let us have the 2 together for £4! So I've said yes.

From OSBERT SITWELL   Renishaw
Thursday, [24/31 March]

My dear Heywood,

I've been meaning to answer you every day, but have had a thousand letters to write and people to see. It was so nice your coming over here – I was furious, after the motor had left, to remember suddenly that I'd never told the driver to charge it to me. But I have done so, and shall be very angry with Anne if she tries to pay me. I had a very licentious letter from Malcolm, as the result of our postcard, full of insinuations, of what sort you can imagine: the sort of letter one has to burn with tongs the moment it arrives.

I go to London Sunday till 22 April or so, thus I fear I shall miss you. But, however unpleasant Matlock is – I mean the course – I'm sure it's better than the stables at WW – I believe W. Smedley[183] was a *tremendous* character, but forget the stories. Try and get up to Stanton-in-the-Peak, above Reresby. It's a lovely place for a walk. A divine village, and moors covered with tumuli. It must be only 2 or 3 miles from Matlock.

I think of you so often with considerable anguish, and hope to see you soon as an officer (I feel I'm talking like your father). 'Tell them who you are!'

Affectionately yours
OSBERT

Oh! The books I've bought.

183 The Smedley of Smedley's Hydro where Heywood was stationed.

Smedley's Hydro
Wednesday, 24 March

Darling,

The registered parcel of socks and vest have come. Not the letter
which you said you'd put in. Maybe it's filtering through. The
course has started hard and furious, and I'm in a fever of anxiety
trying to keep up and understand. I can just grasp it so far, but
made the same stupid mistake all through an exercise this morning
which I fear will go against me. I gather there's no exam, but that
they judge one as one goes along. The majority of them have done
some of it before. I'm unlucky – rather like at Larkhill with the
Charterhouse man – being stuck with this Mackenzie man (whom –
having arrived with – I'm sort of naturally paired off with and sit
next to at all lectures and things) – as he's rather a fool and I don't
like him. It makes a great difference if one gets someone who will
help one with things. He's a very odd man. He suggested going for
a walk yesterday evening, so I went, and then as soon as we got out
he wanted to come back, and didn't want to go down any of the
steep hills, etc. The other two in the room are quite nice, but young
and very much of a pair. There are more officers here than other
ranks, and the majority taking the course are officers. It's like a
liner, and they are 1st class and we are quite a comfortable steerage.
They have a bar and a grander dining room and all that. All the
work so far has been indoors. No sort of PT or anything – so it's
quite opposite to all my previous experiences. By the end of the day
I feel mentally muzzy. There's an enormous amount of stuff to
absorb, and one is meant to do a lot of homework in the evening. I
shall do that, as I want v. much to pass, as it is much more interesting than anything else I've done. 9 out of 10 passed in the last
course, but only 2 out of 10 in the one before that. I have a ghastly
feeling I shan't pass, and I don't think that is just my gloom and
pessimism. I'm sure I could do it, and be quite good at it, with a
little more time, and could pass now if I already knew more of the
groundwork. There are hardly any fatigues – only sweeping the
corridor every 3 days – and hardly any polishing.

I don't quite know yet how much maths. A certain amount but
not so bad as Larkhill. There are about 24 on the course who are
split up into 'syndicates' of 8 who do private work together in a
room. That's where I sit next to Mackenzie. He slightly reminds

me of Jim Knapp-Fisher[184] – only not so nice. It is all rather high class.

A misty day today. I shall now wander out for half an hour. Then work till bedtime. The sort of thing like not being quite sure which of the many things to work at is mixing – and wondering in the middle if one hadn't better open another enormous book. Then there are moments of war horror at all this immensely ingenious complicated paraphernalia. I've just got your No 9 letter. Nothing forwarded yet from Wentworth.

Lots of love. I long to be more bright and cheery to you. If there was just you in this room and we had nothing to do, it would be a perfect place for a holiday. It's odd.

H

From ANNE   10 Warwick Avenue
                     Thursday, 25 March, evening after dinner
Darling Heywood,

Shop was rather worrying somehow today – nothing serious or worth speaking about; but I had not been there for 2 days, and a sort of accumulation met me. Nancy is being *awful* about Hester [Griffin]'s book,[185] talks about sending some back to Secker,[186] and saying down the telephone to them that it was doing very badly with us. *Stopping* in a very subtle way Evelyn Waugh from buying it (who I am certain would have enjoyed it and who *wanted* to buy it, had *asked* for it). Also she's ordered about a dozen of Kate O'Brien's new novel, and is boosting that very much, and sending it to all the prisoners and people in India etc. I did say *Long Division* would be very good for prisoners (it would), and I shall be interested to see if she sends any to any. I shall say more too tomorrow, and tell her that it really is a good recommendable book and that it's not only you and me that thinks so; Raymond [Mortimer] does too: and it's had good reviews in the *New Statesman* and the *Spectator*.

Then Harry [Clifton] wanted 600 copies printed of a letter (completely mad), to be sent to MPs; he was in a *tremendous* hurry, the

184 A publisher friend.
185 Her novel *Long Division* had just come out (under the name Hester Chapman). Heywood and Anne thought it good and very funny; Nancy disagreed.
186 The publishers Secker and Warburg.

day before yesterday. I told Nancy on the telephone to ring up the *Clique* at once, and at 4 *today* she'd done nothing I discovered. She was rather guilty I must say.

Saw a nanny this evening, sent from Mrs Hunt's Agency (who I'd been to on the way to the doctor yesterday). She wants to come, but I took against her rather. Why she wants to is principally because we're so near the Catholic Apostolic Church in Maida Avenue, and one great condition of her coming was that she should be allowed to go to either the 12 or the 5 o'clock two-hour Holy Eucharist every Sunday. I wasn't sure she mightn't be a bit dotty, though she was quite 'nice' and had not bad references. She had tea with Mrs Sternson, and when I asked her (Mrs S.) what she thought, she said at first 'she seems very nice', but when I said I wasn't sure she wouldn't be rather silly, Mrs S. said yes, she had thought she looked a bit vacant sometimes. She said if only young Rossie was older she'd love to look after the baby, and I wish she could, as I think she'd be wonderful.

Fri. morning

Your letter written since the course has come. No, don't try and be 'cheerful' – I don't do I? I do wish I could come to Matlock. Do you know how long the course is?

All love from

ANNE

PS Angela[187] is having a party tonight and Mollie has been asked too. I think I shall ask Mollie to dinner.

From HEYWOOD   Matlock
Saturday, 27 March

Darling Anne,

Got your letter this morning. How dreadful about the quinine, but good about everything else. Wicked Merino. I should buy those two for £4 the pair.

The NAAFI is the old winter garden. A huge glass place still with palms down one side. Badminton in the middle. Darts at one side. The shrill screams of ATs. The high black velvet seats where old ladies used to take waters – now dirty. There are still chains over

187 Angela Culme-Seymour (see Appendix).

the baths for old ladies to pull themselves out by. There's still a list of prices for Turkish baths, etc.

I feel just a little better about the work today. But there is an enormous amount to absorb and it's a drawback not knowing groundwork, like how to make a scale for a map. They rather make one do things without first telling how. Like plotting where photos come on a map on tracing paper. I identified some things in a plot as tanks which were really chicken coops – but so did a good many others. (Better not tell that or anything about the work.) Would it be possible to get Mrs K. to buy me at Rymans a loose-leaf or spring-back cover – above 12 inches tall by 8 wide – larger or smaller wouldn't matter. We get endless bits of paper to keep.

V. little time to write. Hope a longer one tomorrow. Just got your nanny letter. It made me laugh a lot. Great hurry.

Love

H

From ANNE 10 Warwick Avenue
Saturday, 27 March, 4.30 p.m.

Darling Heywood,

Have been sitting indoors all the afternoon instead of walking. Have sorted out the baby's clothes and compared them with lists in books. There seem to be masses. Have also been re-reading Sheila's Dr Gibbon book, and the looking after doesn't sound quite so hopelessly difficult as the first time I read it.

Angela's party last night was for a black conductor whose portrait A. had painted, to show the portrait, which was on an easel; and there were about 6 black people there, including a woman in American Ambulance uniform.

The sad thing was that because he was always so busy talking to other people I was never actually introduced to the conductor, who I thought looked very nice.

The Mollie evening went rather well. Talked about the children and Nancy, whom she's got to like very much I think, which is good. She did though say how odd she was about *Long Division*. Apparently the other day she (Nancy) was saying she could sell any book she wanted to if she tried, so Mollie said, 'Then why don't you start on *L.D.*, and get that pile down a bit?' Nancy said, 'It's the kind of book I despise.'

No other particular news. I'll post this now to get to you Monday. Tonight Coney's coming to dinner.

ANNE

From HEYWOOD   Matlock
                                                      Sunday, 28 March

Darling Anne,

I must try not to ask you little things. But I should like a pr. of thinnish khaki socks if you can spare the coupons. But it's not essential. Also I'd very much like an instrument called a Romer (or Roma). It's a sort of ruler. If you can get it made of talc it would be better, but it doesn't matter. I believe they're difficult to get. I think the best chance is to ring up Sifton Praed in St James's St. Mrs K. could fetch it. If it can be got I'd like it as soon as poss.

How really maddening about Nancy and Hester's book. I should really try to tackle her – as you say. Also about Harry, who is really awfully vital, as one can charge a lot for those jobs of his. Tell her that if he asks for something extraordinary – when you're away – she should write to me – I can often think of how to solve it. And tell her to go slow on new books if we're getting any unsold piles or are very overdrawn.

If walked to Matlock Bath yesterday afternoon – which I sent you the views of. (They don't allow views of here.) It's a v. pretty walk through a valley between sort of cliffs. I went with two others whom I stuck on to. One is very nice. Called Cooper. An artist. He looks a bit like Vivian Macan – the same sort of red nosiness and angularity – but is less slippery and has good sense of humour. He's fed up with the Army and longs to pass this course, and is full of jests. I discovered he'd lived 3 months in Cadgwith[188] which was a link.

The other one – called Reade[189] – is also nice but more difficult and complicated. Has rather a 'fine' face of the thin white intelligent sort. He worked in the Victoria and Albert. Willy [King] might have gossip about him. He doesn't speak very much – then suddenly disapproves of disapproving of the Army in an unconvincing way, and talks about 'red blood' and 'overcoming obstacles',

188 A house which belonged to Heywood's uncle, George Johnstone, and was situated on a cliff top near the village of Cadgwith in Cornwall.
189 See Appendix.

[139]

and how he's sick of the art racket – but at the same time wanting to stay out as long as possible and drink and not go back to work. I should think he's very clever, and doesn't have to bother to work. I wish they were both in the same syndicate as me, so that I could work with them. I get more and more irritated by Mackenzie and could murder him. He had a tremendous hopeless argument this morning with the young man, which was started by him saying he couldn't sleep with a woman who believed in a personal God.

Here, after other army experiences, is rather like being in a convalescent home. Of course the feeling of being judged is very acute, and will probably get more so as the weeks go on. It's awfully sad you can't come here, but I suppose that now it really is wiser not. It would mean 4½ hours jogging each way. The maddening thing is that I believe I could come up for a Sat. night, but think that I too really *must* not as there is so much homework, which can only be done with books which can't be taken away. And I must do my utmost to pass, so that if I do fail I will have no reason to think I might have passed if I had tried more. How dotty it all is, isn't it? One has to be very careful to get things the right way up, and deadly neat – I get so hot and clumsy.

Cooper has got two pictures in some show in the basement of John Lewis. If you ever have a moment do go to see what they look like. I'm now in the syndicate rooms with people sharpening pencils all round.

At Matlock Bath there's a well which petrifies things. They sell the things in the shops. Birds' nests turned to stone etc., probably all bogus. A rude man asked if I had been in the well.

There are a lot of junk shops, very junky. There's no time of course to look at them much.

Awful experiences so many have had in the Army. Of the two men in my room – apart from Mackenzie – one was too near a gun when it exploded, and didn't know what he was doing for a long time after, and was in a home for neurotics for months. The other hurt his leg at PT and they did a dud operation and he is lame for life. Walks with a stick.

I will try to ring you up on Wednesday evening – so send a p.c. if you'll be out. Isn't it hideously uncomfortable now for you – my dear – and do you feel appalled by it all? I believe I dreamed last night that you'd found a nanny.

H

From ANNE 10 Warwick Avenue
Sunday, 28 March, 12.10 p.m.

Darling Heywood,

Lovely sunny day here. Am indoors though, and have only just got up. Listening to Handel's *Messiah* on the wireless – have luckily got down just in time for the best bits. Maggie Tate is singing it. I have it full on and it is deafening and stunning. The awful thing is it's on again from 2.30 till 4.30 and I almost feel I must hear it. But I mustn't, because must work.

Quieter now, Maggie Tate has stopped.

Coney came to dinner last night – took her to Norway which was a success, no one else there, and Norway in very good form. She told us that Debo[190] had had a girl on Friday night at 10 and it had only taken 2 hours. Topolski had left one of her good tarts on his plate and she nearly turned him out, and his new girl had gone into Norway's bedroom without being asked, which was a very rude thing to do. And someone had tried to set her house on fire by putting a tin of phosphorus inside the door.

Coney was very amused by her.

Maggie Tate again.

Bombed Berlin again Mrs Sternson says; what a *bore*. I've told her to put water and biscuits in the shelter[191] and turn off the gas before going to bed. I dare say it is a good thing to be having the baby in the country really, if we persist in bombing Berlin. I find I am now rather looking forward to getting to Ronans.. It is rather tiresome at the shop now, my neither being quite in nor out of it, and it's not being worth starting cataloguing the old books which I so wanted to do. I wish Craig [Macfarlane] would write about the lease[192] as I am rather worried about it.

It is awful how long it is till I see you again. I calculate that the baby is due on Wednesday in a month. If it comes then you might perhaps come for that weekend, say a month next Friday. I thought you might stay at Ronans and bicycle out to see me, as it would

190 Nancy's youngest sister, now Duchess of Devonshire.
191 Heywood's father had given them a shelter. It was in the basement and was supposed to be able to withstand the weight of the house falling on top of it. It had four bunks and later a kitchen drawer for the baby to sleep in.
192 The lease of the shop, a seven-year one, was to expire in September 1943. The landlord allowed it to be extended for a few months, to give more time to find somewhere else. Finally, the shop moved to 10 Curzon Street, where it still is now.

be nice being there in the evenings etc. The baby coming in between makes our seeing each other again seem almost as remote as
next year. Debo's baby was a fortnight late, and she's had to pay
her nursing home 60 guineas before being there at all, for nothing
(so a week from the time it was due). On the other hand, Mrs
Sternson says of all the people she knows who have had babies, she
doesn't know one who was late, and all were punctual or early.
Ruth [Gathorne-Hardy] and Betty [Mylius][193] were early. I don't
know about Sheila and Fidelity.

All love

ANNE

Anne was invited by Peta Lambe to spend the nights at Ronans to
avoid the bombing of London that was expected to follow the
Allied bombing of Berlin. She went on the evening of 29 March and
commuted to the shop by train twice, returning to Warwick Avenue
on the 31st.

From ANNE   Ronans
Monday, 29 March

Darling Heywood,

Well, here I am at Ronans. Rather pleasant I must say. The bore
though is that I feel quite *certain* the raid won't be tonight, and I have
to go up to London tomorrow to my dentist. (Otherwise I could have
brought work down here to do.) I can't put him off, it would mean
paying a guinea; also he would never be able to see me again before
the baby (I've already had to wait 3 weeks). It was embarrassing
coming here somehow, especially with Mrs Sternson.[194] I told her
that you had rung up and *insisted* on my going.

I had a nice breakfast this morning with 2 letters from you and
the book of views. I will certainly go to John Lewis and see
Cooper's picture. Augustus John has a picture there too that
someone was going to see.

The course must be very worrying. I'm afraid the file thing I sent
was the wrong sort and spiked instead of spring-clipping. I didn't

193 A great friend of the Hills, wife of Victor (Bobby) Mylius.
194 Embarrassing to be leaving London because of a possible raid, when the Sternsons
with their two children weren't doing this, and couldn't have if they'd wanted to.

discover it till it had gone (I'd got one for myself too.) I'll get the right sort though. Are there no books it might be useful to have?

No pants or parcel of any kind has come from any shop.

A nanny rang up this morning who'd seen the *Daily Telegraph* advertisement on Friday. I'm seeing her Wednesday. I thought her voice sounded rather nice, and am hopeful.

My head calculations about the baby are quite wrong. I find when I look at the calendar it will be next Sunday 4 weeks (2 May).

Tues. In train on the way to London

Of course there haven't been raids. After hours of indecision I've decided to go to Ronans tonight, but back to Warwick Ave. Tomorrow *whatever* happens. Especially as Charles [Lambe] says they can't use more than 40 bombers now.

Ronans, in bed. Tuesday evening, 30.3.43

It was nice talking to you (the Lambes being there made me feel rather self-conscious though, and that I ought to be saying 'Darling' more than we do).

All well at shop. Felt sheepish over having been here (though Nancy, when Peta [Lambe] rang up, had nicely encouraged me to go, and made it easy). I concealed at the shop that I was coming back again tonight. Without lying I just didn't mention it.

I think I'll go back home tomorrow (I want to rather now) and stay in London as long as there's a raging gale, like now, and come here again if there's a wonderful clear calm moonlight night.

Wednesday morning

Very pleasant here lying in bed in the morning with the sun pouring in. I look forward more and more to my holiday here, and think it will be idyllic. I shall be so important too which will be fun. It will probably pour with rain all the time, the weather being so wonderful now, but even so.

I was thinking, it was rather ridiculous yesterday, I was half as long in the train during the day (going to and coming from the shop) as if I'd gone to Matlock.

I brought home John [Hill]'s pictures[195] yesterday. (Having no luggage to carry it was easy.) I thought I'd put them in the sitting

195 Four watercolours of Glengariff Castle, Bantry Bay, painted while on holiday there in 1937.

room again, and various sitting-room ones in the nursery and bedroom. I thought I must get all the nursery ones hung before there's a nanny to object.

Time to get up to catch train. Extraordinary that next time you're at W. Ave. there'll (presumably) be a baby in the nursery.

Fondest love from
ANNE

From HEYWOOD

Matlock
Tuesday, 30 March

Darling Anne,

I'm glad you went to Ronans. I was in a fever when I heard about the raid, and getting the telegram was a great relief. I haven't heard yet if there was a raid or not in London.

Life here is rather like swinging on a rope over a chasm, or drowning and clutching on to floating wood. I think I am still just all right, but might drown at any moment, and one can't tell. We had to be seen by an oculist this morning, to find out if we had stereo vision, and I had to look at a line of aeroplanes on a diagram to see if any stood out, and none did, so I had to rest and then look again and again, and at last they did.

I haven't read a line of anything but work so far – the week I've been here. I think you'd better keep Huxley's book[196] ready for me.

I've just heard we bombed Berlin again last night. I'm going to wire to you to stay at Ronans. I've forgotten the telephone number.

I go for little half-hour potters in the evening before starting homework so as to get fresh air. It's Smedley's *Hydro* not Hotel. The W means Wing.

No time – no time –

Love, my darling, I'm always thinking about you.

H

From ANNE

10 Warwick Avenue
Wednesday, 31 March

Darling Heywood,

A great revolution took place today. After the nanny had gone I

196 Aldous Huxley, *The Art of Seeing*.

went down to see what the Sternsons had thought of her, and when I said, 'What do you think of her?' there was an embarrassed silence from Mrs S. Finally Mr S. said he thought that to cook 3 meals a day for a nanny as well as me was going to be too much for Mrs S. and she wouldn't be able to do it, and it would be far easier for her to look after the baby. So we're not going to have a nanny after all. Mrs Saunders will come in daily and wash nappies and wash up supper and clean kitchen and other work to make up for a bit for the extra Mrs S. will be doing.

My feelings about it are mixed. On one hand I will obviously have to do rather more myself; for instance it will have to sleep with me. But she suggested that when you come on leave it can sleep with her. And it will be all right leaving it for occasional weekends – she said that. And she says if I ever want to go away for a weekend with it, she'd like to come too; 'it would make a change' she said. (She seems to think that Mr S., Marlene and Rossie could manage for the weekend by themselves quite all right.)

The boring thing now is ever having moved out of the old bedroom, and the Green and Abbott[197] bill that it will cost. And all the nursery preparations turning out to be unnecessary. And the £s on advertising being wasted. But still, £s in the future will be saved. I'll have to pay Mrs Sternson and Mrs Saunders between them about what I'd pay a nanny I think, but will save a nanny's food, laundry and gas, probably about £70 or £80 a year.

Mr Sternson had a rather charming argument in favour of the new arrangement, that there is a good deal of pleasure as well as work in looking after a baby, but none at all in cooking for a nanny. I think all the nannies must have shown off and been rather awful at their teas in the kitchen.

Fondest love from
ANNE

From ANNE · 10 Warwick Avenue
Thursday evening, 1. 4. 43

Darling Heywood,

The course sounds wildly agitating. I think it is wonderful to compete at all, and to have stereo eyes.

197 See Appendix under John and Sheila Hill.

I am well. Have had rather a day of bouts of inward agitations, doubts, depressions, worries, anxieties and longings for you to be home again, but feel better this evening. Thoughts of the shop and the baby alternately worry me to death. Don't *you* worry over this though, as this fussing only happens in bouts, and does not last. I know for instance that I won't worry a bit at Ronans, almost certainly. Also all the 3 nanny sister-in-laws[198] have been very consoling on the telephone this evening, and cheered me greatly, and will all come and help, and set me and Mrs Sternson going. In a way, perhaps having both shop and baby is a good thing, as when I'm immersed in one I stop thinking of the other, and the two together do probably stop me brooding over missing you like I might if alone in the country with nothing to do.

About Nancy, the thing is we are really tremendously lucky to have someone who can manage at all, and Nancy does manage in a rough and ready way all right, and indeed sometimes has spectacular successes far beyond my powers, and will I believe get better and better.

Questions: 1 Diana Beaumont wants to sell the Avon Shakespeare, Kegan Paul, 1912, no notes, 12 vols., excellent condition. How much shall we offer? (This is Nancy's description.) 2 A man doing an investigation into the domestic sculpture of the country houses of Durham and Northumberland for Durham University wants to know if he can have a print of one of the pictures in *CHB*;[199] the Lumley Castle Stucco group. Where are the plates?

Tomorrow am going to *The Merry Widow* with Sheila, John, Ruth, Jonny, Nic, Jo and Mollie. Ruth and Jonny are staying here.

Fondest love from
ANNE

When does your course end?

---

198 Anne's three sisters-in-law were Heywood's sister Sheila Hill, Anne's elder brother Jock's wife, Fidelity Cranbrook, and her youngest brother Antony's wife, Ruth Gathorne-Hardy. All three had had nannies for their first babies and all were now without.

199 *Country House Baroque*. A book published by the shop in 1940, with photographs by Antony Ayscough, an introduction by Sacheverell Sitwell, and a descriptive text by Margaret Jourdain.

From HEYWOOD   Matlock
                                Thursday, 1 April 1943, 6 p.m.
Darling,
   Your letter has at last been forwarded from Wentworth with the
10/-. A very 'good' letter and it came last night – during a day of
absolute brain-splitting work – which went on without stop from 9
a.m. till 10 p.m. I had a raging headache by the end and felt full of
gloom as my work seemed so much worse than everyone else's. My
map was spidery and inaccurate, and all the others had made wonderful clear bold plans.[200] And then there was an awful thing of
working out scales. It's fairly simple arithmetic really, but I think
my brain has gone, as in *Hangover Square*.[201] It clicks and *won't*
work. It's hell – every single day of the Army having some new
frightful obstacle. It's such a tearing wearing strain and I long for a
relax. I now think it would be better to be an officer because there is
sometimes more chance of being alone. Having lived in our little
world . . .
   Here another day began and now is over – but there's time for
post. A less bad day and I'm feeling better.
   The file is all right if you haven't sent another. Cooper is nice and
a great standby. Mackenzie gets worse and worse.
   Imagine me with a ruler, a roma, a protractor, dividers, and
tracing paper, pins, stereorules, plots . . .
                                                     Love
                                                       H

From ANNE   Friday, 2 April
Darling Heywood,
   Am in the shop, feeling not miserable at all but rather bored and
lazy. Gradually clearing on and round my desk, finishing off little
tasks by slow degrees, and writing informative things down for
Mollie and Nancy (which they'll never look at I expect). I shall
really probably not be away from the shop very much longer than
we used to be when we had long long holidays.
   Nancy has redone the window without a *Long Div*, I found this

200 '. . . [it is an] undeniable fact that in Cor. D. Division [at Eton] the stupidest boys
did the best maps, the Collegers always the worst. I wonder why.' *The Lyttelton
Hart-Davis Letters* [vol. 1] *1955–56*, John Murray, 1978, p. 14.
201 Novel by Patrick Hamilton.

morning, which I rectified; and I sold 2 at lunch time which I shall point out soon.

Poor Knole [picture framer] has been in twice pathetically in the last month – he is in the Mile End Road. I'm giving him some little cat drawings I found in the bathroom nest of drawers, to passe-partout (not much of an order, but there isn't anything else to be done).

Splendid, *Mollie* has just commented to Nancy on my *Long Division* sales. Nancy has over-said How Splendid, as if it was some awful old thing one was stuck with, and that it was very clever to sell.

This will have to be your Monday morning letter I think, as tomorrow there'll be the shop in the morning, and I'm having lunch with Janetta,[202] and will walk home probably afterwards, by which time it will be about post time. I'm having tea with Jim [Lees-Milne] again on Sunday. Otherwise I have no arrangements. Will probably go out on Tues. night as that is Mr Sternson's night off.

Much love from
ANNE

From HEYWOOD   Matlock
Friday and Saturday, 2nd and 3 April

Darling,

I broke off abruptly yesterday, as was called for by Cooper and Reade to go for a walk. I meant to go for only half an hour, and then come back to work. But I stayed out for two hours, (though I worked for an hour till bedtime when I got back). There are Satans who stand beckoning the wrong way. They use all the nice arguments about it being bad for you to do any more now. We went up a pretty valley – cascades and ruins. Then we had some beer in a pub. Then the thing about supper began, as it always does in the Army, and one can't decide. They said they'd go down to the Olde England Hotel and I said I'd go back to work. They said it would be bad for me and I said well, I'd got to eat anyhow so I might as well come, although I knew the nice long dawdle it would mean. It's down the very steep hill to Olde England. They said no. The people here aren't as nice as the Yorkshire ones. Maybe they're

202 Janetta Woolley (see Appendix).

sophisticated from old Hydro days, or else just fed up with soldiers. So then we went to the Queen's. No again, so we had some more beer. No at the Crown. No at the Railway Inn. More beer and more beer. So enter the squalid hut of the forces canteen, but Reade was pushed by someone in the queue, and it was all horrid, so we remembered the cinema café, so we went there. That had shut at 7. So we ended up at the Church Army halfpenny sandwich bar – rather weak and giggling. It's a great thing having buddies. Reade is in a way the more interesting – lazy and cynical and enigmatic and silent and a bit rude, and one doesn't know what he's thinking. He's the sort of person one wants to be liked by – whereas Cooper is cosier.

Saturday

Have now had your revolution letter and another this morning. Wonderful you are writing. I was deeply interested by the revolution. Can well feel all your feelings about it. I feel the same. I fear about it meaning too much for you to do – but I think that not having the nanny-presence will be a great relief. She'd have always been on top of you, and would have had to have been so splendid not to have been a fret. We might tell the Orchards it's an economy? If it doesn't work we could get the nanny later. If it does work, it will bind the Sternsons to us. You are quite right about Nancy. She is very splendid in many ways, and also is an antidote to our own failings.

Yesterday was another terrific one of work. Right up to 11 at night. One gets absolutely exhausted trying to decide what tiny pin-like things in photos are. What seems a tank may easily be a camel. And then you have to write very clear concise reports, and you mustn't guess. And it's so difficult not to put possibly, probably or might. I can't truthfully decide myself whether if I pass I would be good at the job or not. I should think the chances of my passing are honestly about 3 to 1 against.

The course goes on for another 3 weeks from today – as far as I can gather. I don't think we'll leave here till the middle of the week after. Whether I pass or not I have to go back to Wentworth for a bit – I believe – which is hell. If I don't pass I might then have to go back to Larkhill – but it's unpredictable.

Two from my room have gone off for 36 hours, and Reade's wife is coming down. I feel jealous, and so long to see you, but it's impossible. So I'll be alone with Mackenzie tonight. Am now in fact. He's just arranged himself in the window in the sun. Every morning he has a bath, and then sits naked on his bed staring. I think he thinks his figure is good. His face is revolting. He's not queer. Reade said he had seen me before and couldn't remember where. Then he suddenly did remember. We once in the shop had some eighteenth-century watercolour drawings of ceilings, and I took them to the V & A, and it was he who saw me. Pleasing of him to remember.

I think next week will be crammed with work, and I'll only be able to write odd snatches. I've got to know what every different type of Panzer, naval boat, aeroplane, every horrible thing looks like from the air. An exercise on working out map scales is what I most dread.

This is a nice Osbert[203] isn't it? Did you ever send the 12/6? I believe you didn't. I long for you to get to Ronans, so that you can sink back. I am so futilely preoccupied with my own idiotic worries that I don't think of all yours nearly enough. I can't somehow believe in the baby yet.

Mackenzie has now changed into pyjamas and trousers and is lying with his horrid breast exposed.

Could I have two hanks?

Love darling
HEYWOOD

I can't read Osbert's PS.

From ANNE   10 Warwick Avenue
                                    Sunday morning, 4 April
Darling Heywood,
    Wonderful amazing day. I am lying without stockings in the long chair in John's garden[204] boiling in the sun. I have just taken the geraniums out of the cellar. Four of them are alive but they have been in the cellar too long, and though some of them have got quite tall, they are snow-white instead of green. They'll get all right I think though. Morogh is having an awful time with three children

203 Letter from him.
204 John and Sheila lived in Maida Avenue. The end of their garden adjoined Heywood's and Anne's at right angles. They had had an opening made in the wall between.

in the next door garden. They keep talking to him and asking him questions, and he is politely answering. 'What is a fork?' 'A fork is a thing with several sharp points for digging in the ground', etc. He is obviously tremendously bored.

I do hope you are having time off for a nice walk or something. The course sounds a *nightmare*, and I do wish I could see you. How much longer is it? Lionel [Perry][205] says if you pass you'll probably go to or near Oxford afterwards.

It is a mystery about the Matlock letters, as I think there are still 2 or 3 I first wrote, before the week's leave, that you never got. One with a wad of Bromo[206] in it.

A shock suddenly – the 1 o'clock news, and I thought it was only 12. I had forgotten about the clocks changing.

My dear, could you write to your bank and get them to send you a new cheque book and sign some and send me them. As I can't find yours, and today will *have* to pay all the bills, income tax, Gas Light & Coke Co., and so on, with my own cheques and I haven't anything in the bank. But it won't matter overdrawing for a bit if you've lost your cheque book or anything.

The Merry Widow with the children was fun; they looked much older and bigger and were very funny. It was a good choice for them, as there were things like a revolving stage, and they were fascinating to watch watching it. I hardly saw Sheila, as we all separated immediately after to get the children to bed. She's coming to stay on Thursday though. Ruth has volunteered to look after the baby at Glemham for a month or 6 weeks before Xmas, so that I shall be able to work late at the shop then, which will be wonderful. Everybody seems to think that it will be all right the baby being looked after by Mrs Sternson and me, but that I ought to have a monthly nurse for the first fortnight or so at home. So I shall ring up the doctor and try. If I can't, either Ruth, Sheila or Fidelity will come and stay, they say.

Nancy, me, Topolski, Patrick[207] and several other people all

205 A charming Irishman who was a great friend of Anne and Heywood.
206 Make of tracing-paper-like lavatory paper, the best, now defunct due to technological advances in this field.
207 They were all neighbours: Nancy lived in Blomfield Road on the Regent's Canal, almost opposite John and Sheila in Maida Avenue; Feliks Topolski lived opposite Anne and Heywood, in a studio looking onto the canal basin (the row of houses there long since demolished); and Patrick Kinross lived at 4 Warwick Avenue, three doors down from Anne and Heywood.

wrote to the Mayor of Paddington about the pollarding of the planes along the canal (Nancy was told by someone that it is quite the wrong time of year to pollard, and also that it's being done very unskilfully and may kill them). Yesterday an answer came saying that the Mayor had ordered the cutting to be stopped while there was an investigation, so that is rather splendid.

I haven't forgotten about your socks but they are rather difficult to get in your size. Go on asking me for things as I *like* getting them. Even when I'm at Ronans, I shall still be able to, as I shall be going to Bracknell now and then. And at Windsor I shall get Mama to; she'd rather enjoy it.

Much love, darling Heywood, from

ANNE

I do long for you continuously more than I can say. On mornings like this for instance. I so want you to be in the garden with me now, this moment.

From ANNE   In the sun in the garden
                                              Monday morning, 5 April

Darling Heywood,

Wonderful long letter from you today. I am very glad that Cooper and Reade do force you out for walks and amusements sometimes, as I think it is true and not Satanic that you will work better after a relax. I believe it's been proved by experiments. You might have a breakdown otherwise. That might be a good thing of course, but it would probably be very unpleasant.

Yes, I am increasingly pleased about the new arrangements here really. Especially as I go on getting letters from nannies, and they all have phrases like 'I do want to be with someone who likes their babies to look well-cared-for', and about being C. of E.

I too feel exactly the same as you say you do, that I don't think enough of what a dreadful time *you're* having, but almost exclusively about my own little difficulties and problems. So it cancels itself out, and allows us both to be entirely selfish, and means we can grumble, moan and complain to each other as much as we like.

I must do some work now. If only you were in the shop everything would be ideal for me. I should do a little light shop work in the garden (as I'm going to do now) and be nearly entirely carefree. As it is I have misgivings about the shop when I'm not there. I'm going there this afternoon, to look at reports[208] and collect bills to be paid. I'm trying to pay all the publishers etc. before leaving.

£25 has come from Father this morning, so it really is all right about the allowance. Isn't it a relief? We must thank him a *lot*. I have told him in my letter about the no-nanny economy. Not that it really will be much economy with the extra I'll be paying Mrs S., and the daily nappy washer. Still I suppose besides the food and fuel, a nanny would probably need all sorts of ironing boards and special aprons, special saucepans, little cupboards and buckets and baskets, all kinds of extraordinary things I'm sure.

Rossie tramples the garden and spoils things a good deal but I'm not going to say or do anything, whatever he does. For one thing, I think Mr Sternson's digging and liming does more good to the garden than Rossie does harm; and what*ever* harm Rossie could possibly do will be far more than made up for by having nice Mrs S. for the baby, I now think).

There are no hankies I fear, as the laundry hasn't been for nearly 3 weeks, but here is some gauze.

Fondest love from

ANNE

From ANNE   Tuesday, 6 April

Darling Heywood,

Having a very late lunch at Ruggieri's (2.30); rather horrid place. But the waitresses, who used to be nasty, rude and take no notice, are friendly and nice now they see my 'condition', and serve me quickly and smile a lot.

Lucky I went to the shop this morning. John Gielgud came in and asked if we had anything on costume. Nancy said no. I found 3 things. (He didn't buy them.) Then he said had we any books about Italy. Nancy said NO. (She never qualifies her noes, or tries to think at all.) I went to the drawer and brought out the *Campi Phlegraei*[209] plates, and he was *delighted* with those and bought 4 at 10/- each. He also bought a book about the funeral of Queen Anne for £3. 10/-. I'm sure he'd have just left the shop if I hadn't been there. Then I sold that Dutch book you've just bought – plates of some sort of

208 *Clique* reports, answers on books for which they advertised.
209 Sir William Hamilton, *Campi Phlegraei: Observations on the Volcanoes of the Two Sicilies* (1776).

pageant and various things – cost £4 marked £7. 10/- to Eisemann. For only £6 – he bargained away and I was a bit weak. Do you think it's a pity? We've done well lately over somebody's wedding – that nice set of Tennyson (white and red) for £4. 4/- (me again – I pushed it in front of someone just nearly leaving in despair), and quite a lot of odd pictures, flower books and objects to various people, and the mahogany card box with counters to Bill Astor.

You said something to Osbert about exchanging a Fester book of his for that £12 one of ours. What *did* you say? How much? No one knows. He's been in. Answer please.

Later at home

A great bore – this is the night I'm supposed to go out, and I had meant to wait till the Sternsons had gone and then cook myself an egg downstairs in the kitchen. Now it's 8.15 and they don't seem to be going. I *can't* go out now, and will just have to starve if they don't (it's too late and I had planned not to and don't want to).

Later

I solved the difficulty by toasting the bread left over from tea on the gas fire, and opening a tin of sardines from the cupboard (that I'd bought a day or two ago, and not taken to the kitchen). And the new chocolate ration.

My new Allowance Book has come too, and I got £7 from the Post Office with it, quite nice. There's lots more to come.

If you ever have a chance of buying anything for the shop, we rather need things for people to give as wedding presents – 'good' conventional sets and bindings, that sort of thing. Remembering that very often people have to give wedding presents to people they hardly know.

I failed with Oliver [Messel] today, who is doing the decor for a ballet about 1790 in St Petersburg. Wanted pictures of Russian uniforms of that date – or women's clothes – have we anything? Someone else wanted any book with pictures of Paris during the Revolution – people at the barricades. How I *long* to know our stock properly, and how I hope that Nancy stays and that I shall be able to learn it in the autumn. I shall make the most wonderful card index of our stock if Nancy does stay. I shall combine it with punctual stock-taking.

If PIW *stands* for Photographic Interpretation Wing, I don't see

that it matters saying you do PI (I haven't though to be safe –
except to Elizabeth Glenconner, who had said , 'Oh, he's at Matlock, is he? Philip [Toynbee] did Photographic Interpretation there.'
She couldn't remember if he passed or failed). Or does it stand for
Primary Intelligence?

Love
ANNE

From HEYWOOD   Matlock
[postmarked Wednesday, 7 April]

Darling,

I had a nice restoring weekend going for two walks in the lovely
weather. The country is odd here – because it doesn't always feel
like country, but more like a big park in a town, because of the
black trees and dust – but that is pretty.

We had a v. hard day yesterday. I worked till quarter to 12 and
some went on till 2 in the morning. So I'm feeling jaded today. But
in spite of the effort I wish it was longer here, as it's sure to be
worse afterwards. What day do you go to Ronans? Could I possibly
have £3 – so that I don't have to keep on asking. Registered. No
great hurry.

Cooper said that the sergeant in his last unit called him Decayed
Gentry. Reade told Cooper that he was sure he lived in Earls Court.

And could you get Mrs S. to send me a vest about once a week
when you're away and ask her to pack it in paper and string that I
can use again.

The American officers are amusing in class. They put up their
hands and say 'Question'. I haven't yet asked a single question. I'm
now in the 'Syndicate' room waiting for some exercises to be given
us. After that I'll have to stop at once. It's a v. difficult place to get
supper in the evening. The only place possible is Lilybank Hydro –
which is fascinating in its way. Packed tight with old ladies – all
talking about their ailments and cures. We talked to an ex-maid of
here in a pub, and she said there were terrible scenes when the old
ladies had to leave here at ten days' notice. None of them knew
where to go, and several of them died.

Now the exercise is over. It was putting contours on a map,
which I'm particularly bad at, and my result was palsied and
ghastly.

I can't help sinking back into reading *Horizon*.[210] I've hardly read a line of anything yet, except I did manage to read Osbert's bit on Sunday.

Love

H

From ANNE   10 Warwick Avenue
                                           Monday, 7 April

Darling H,

Didn't go to the shop today. To the doctor in the morning where I had to wait for hours. I have to go again the Monday I go to Ronans (next Monday week). He described to me the symptoms of labour so that I should know. He said the baby was small so far, and unless it grows enormously during the next few weeks I should not have too bad a time. My blood pressure is rather low but I am otherwise very well. He thought the chance of my getting a monthly nurse for when I come home is minute, but he would try. He had various stories about the tremendous shortage of nurses.

Ate at the Dutch Kitchen in Baker Street on the way home, where the food is rather good. Then worked rather ineffectively and lazily and interruptedly at home till about 9, when I washed my hair, set and dried it, which lasted almost till bedtime.

During a part of the afternoon I read Sheila's baby book and came to where he said, 'I should like to record here my profound admiration for the work of the nurses trained by the Mothercraft Training Society', so I rang up the MTS and asked if they had a nurse who would come to me for a week or 2 from about 24 May. They said they thought one of their nurses would be free then, and gave me her name and address. So I have written to her. I hope very much she will be able to come, as I think it would make a great difference if Mrs Sternson and I could be shown *in the house* the things to do, by someone like that, who would set us going in an authoritative way, on a routine. Otherwise I should have to show Mrs S. in my fumbling way the things the nursing home nurses had shown me, and I should feel diffident too, Mrs S. already having brought up 2. Also it would be very nice not to have the baby in my room for the first fortnight.

210 The magazine edited by Cyril Connolly.

Thursday morning

Just had rather a sad disappointment. Mr Sternson had discovered that all this time we should have been emptying the lodger's gas meter, and calculated that there should be between £15 and £20 in it. So I left a note for Tony asking if she had the key of it (2 days ago). This morning she called me and said they hadn't a key, but she'd been able to open it without one, and would I come up and count what was in it. So I did, and there was only 10/-. I could scarcely hide my chagrin. Quite obviously some workman has discovered the no key thing and taken a mass, as £5. 10/- for a whole year is only about 2/- a week, which is impossibly little. Mr S. says I must ring the Gas Co. And get a key.

Fondest love

ANNE

From ANNE   10 Warwick Avenue

Thursday, 8 April, in bed 9.30 p.m.

Darling H,

Was at the shop all day today. Nothing very outstanding happened.

There is what looks as if it's going to be a wonderful book about Etty coming out. £5. 5/-, £4. 4/- to pre-publication subscribers. We are sending out a mass of prospectuses to people. I'll send you a prospectus. Nancy is keen on it.

Who is Major Jordan, who lives in Oxford? He wrote saying he wanted a good set of prints on some architectural subject, say Old London. Of course I wrote back about the Ackermanns. I quoted the glowing description in that book about colour plate books. We only seem to have 26 left now – I told him we sold them at a guinea each, but he could have the 26 for £18. Is that too little? I said a complete set would probably cost £90 or £100 – I don't know if that was really right at all, but I risked it.

I think I shall ask Nancy to forward all the letters of that type to me – and say I would like to be kept well in touch during my confinement. She might forward some of that type of letter to you, and some to me, straight away. What do you think? *Answer*, please.

I'm always asking you important questions which you *never* answer. There were some the other day and I can't remember what they were.

[157]

It is extraordinary how this baby is coming at *exactly* the most convenient time of year for the shop, so that I was not too pregnant at Xmas, and it should be well weaned and (I hope) quite old and strong by next Xmas. And it is lucky to have this fortnight still at the shop in April, as such a mass of vital Income Tax and those typing things come in April.

Sheila is staying here tonight, but I haven't seen her yet – she has gone to a play with Miss Cocke.[211] Nancy is having dinner with Hester [Griffin] tomorrow night which is rather interesting. I don't *quite* think it will be a success, do you? Nancy will be rather mocking and patronising I think, but perhaps not. (I don't mean *to* her, but about her afterwards.)

The pair of Sitwells came in today and O. said to me in front of a rather nice shy new customer 'Have you ever thrown any customer out physically?' Of course she thought it was some kind of reference to her, and that perhaps we might all 3 be going to. She was very brave and steeled herself to outstay us but was obviously shattered.

We have no more copies of *Country House Baroque* at all. Osbert wants one. Or do you think there might be some somewhere? Mrs Kentall has looked all through the packing room.

Nancy says Alice Harding's husband has left her and is living with a man, and that A. Harding wrote to Mr Harding saying he must choose between the man and her. The man answered saying Mr Harding had chosen him.

I don't know if you read in the paper, about Sir Somebody Laurie who was find £500 for having both a civilian and an Army ration book. That really was a queer case – he was given away about the ration books by the man he lived with, because (being very important) he had had a soldier, whom the man he lived with was in love with, sent to Tunisia. No other news.

Fondest love

ANNE

From HEYWOOD Matlock

Friday, 9 April

Darling Anne,

I've been bad this week. I was very bad yesterday when we

211 Miss Cocke (pronounced Coke) worked for John Hill at Green & Abbott (see Appendix).

stopped work at 4.30, and I went out to tea with C. & R. and then I meant to come back to write to you and to work, but I went to a bad cinema with them, then we went to a pub, and sat drinking on till bedtime.

I don't think there was ever anything definite with Osbert about exchanging that book. He has got a not so nice copy as ours and he wants ours instead. I never made any price. Do you think say £10?

What splendid shop things you've been doing. That Goncourt book is about the French Revolution, so are those little *Almanachs des Prisons*. I haven't time to buy things here – and there's nothing to buy. I might go into Buxton on Sat. with C. & R. and will look about there. I enjoyed your letter very much. Those coloured views of country houses could be 5/- or 10/-. As you think.

I'm in a quandary what to do about leave, whether to apply for baby leave as soon as I finish here. I believe in snatching anything as soon as poss. Or else it may be imposs: but if I was there in your crisis time – it mightn't be a good idea. Ponder – and I'll ring up on Monday night. I have to apply for anything like leave by writing to Wentworth before 19th.

Last night Mackenzie produced remarkable photos. Professional, like Charles [Lambe]'s and Victor [Stiebel]'s[212] only larger and better. A good many were obscene and some vulgar. The eye of a cat and the navel of a woman – that was one of the better ones. I think he's spent a lot of time with women in Morocco on flat roofs – like a horrid sort of modern Omar Khayyam. But the photos are good photos.

Love

H

From HEYWOOD   Matlock
Saturday, 10 April, 6 p.m.

Darling,

Feeling rather melancholic this evening. This great long vista of boredom and fright ahead, and I can't see how it will ever end or when I shall get back to be with you. There are a great many desolate moments of hopelessness. Though tonight's wasn't so bad

212 A well-known dress designer. Brian Reade described Mackenzie as 'a male chauvinist, a frightful joke of a person, who showed us erotic drawings of his, done "under the bedclothes", or so he said'.

as it has sometimes been – in fact it was also just fairly enjoyable as we were sitting in the huge old winter garden, which still has its old hydro lampshades (though there are holes in them) – they give a dusty dim light – and a soldier playing the piano on the stage and the echoing voices of a few ATs, and Cooper and me drinking tea and eating a nasty fishcake and having nothing more to say to each other.

The afternoon wasn't a success. Reade had wanted to go to Buxton which was 20 miles away, but that meant leaving before lunch (official work stops at 10 on Saturday) and Cooper and I said we must do our own work till lunchtime, and then we would go to a place called Bakewell and walk back through Haddon Hall by the river. So we did that, but Reade sulked and didn't speak and it was difficult for any of us to speak. It was a grey cold day and blank. I felt sorry for Reade and how silly we must seem, and I wanted really to go to Buxton because there might be some antique shops and because it's a spa and there's a crescent. But Reade's the sort of person who can pass things without doing any work.

The work is boiling up to the fury I expected. Imagine having to recognise a pinpoint on a photo taken at thousands of feet. The pinpoint is a gun and you've got to know whether it's German or English and which of the thousand sorts it is. You can't tell because you can't see, so you've got to know which of the 100 tractors might pull a particular gun. Perhaps you can't see the tractor – so you've got to know what it all might measure – but you don't know the scale of the photo so you've got to work that out. But the gun is measured in metres and so you've got to change inches to metres. Then there aren't enough measuring things to go round the class – and you've got to finish in an hour. I'm sinking fast I fear. This next week we've got all the air forces and all the navies to do – as just a part of the schedule. Of course most people already know the different sorts of British aeroplanes – Oh heavens.

You scold me about not answering questions. I *know*. The thing is I have to snatch the time to write, and often I can't find or have time to look at your letter just then. It does help if you underline questions. It must sound as if there's lots of time what with the walks and the melancholy, but there is not. I couldn't begin to answer shop letters. I'm not being peevish but just wanting you to be sorry for me which you anyhow are. Isn't it appalling – when

Heywood in bookshop back room, 1939

ABOVE *Frances and Ralph Partridge.* BELOW *Their house, Ham Spray.*

ABOVE *Heywood and Anne.* BELOW *Lawrence Gowing and Julia Strachey.*

Peta Lambe

Derek Hill, 1936

Hester Griffin

Jonny Gathorne-Hardy, 1943

Nancy Mitford and Anne

Viva King

Malcolm Bullock and Osbert Sitwell

Jim McKillop outside 17 Curzon Street, 1940

ABOVE *Matlock, 1943: Heywood middle of back row; Mackenzie (with moustache) second from left middle row, with Cooper and Brian Reade on his left.* BELOW, LEFT *Dorothy Cranbrook at Snape.* RIGHT *The house from the outside.*

Heywood with Harriet

Books old and new, antiques, prints and bibelots—the war has brought a quickened appreciation of these things and there's much knowledgeable buying. Heywood Hill's bookshop in Curzon Street, magnet for bibliophiles, has attracted these two girls. The one on the left wears Strassner's jacket-dress printed in a white formal pattern on navy, perennially crisp for summer. It is gathered at the waist, falls in soft folds. The girl on the right wears Rahvis's narrowly belted red and green print of polo players and horses' heads, pouch-pleated at the bodice. Models will be copied with necessary modifications

this is the moment of all moments that I should be dreadfully sorry for you. Darling – I am – I hope – I pray I am – but I know I love you.

And there you'll be this week gathering up the cots and the nappies and moving heavily about and remembering and forgetting millions of tiny things.

Sunday morning

I want to tear up this last night's letter with its confusion and sentiment but I won't. If those pants still haven't come could you try to ring up the place. I *think* it is called AUSTINS and it's in Shaftesbury Avenue. 3 pairs and I paid with a cheque. And another vest this week. I know you'll have so much to do this week – so don't bother if no time.

Morogh wrote to me about that picture of his. I've no idea where it is. I'll send him a p.c. Have only dim memories of it and had forgotten that he left it with us – if he really did. I don't know Major Jordan. I should make him pay before – if he buys those things. The price is all right for the Ackermanns – not less.

I *know* that there are some CHBs somewhere, and I thought they were in the basement. I think we got 50 bound not long ago (from Unwins). There are no dust wrappers for them.

I used to know the man who sneaked about Laurie, called Capron. The most terrific active snob I've ever known. I was about the first rung on his ladder at Cambridge, and through me he got to know Etonians and then on to Lords. He lived a long time with some old countess – a relation of Morogh's – who left him money when she died.

Did anything come of the nurse? Very cute of you to think of ringing up that place.

Love
H

From ANNE   10 Warwick Avenue
                                                Saturday, 16 April
Darling H,

Am just back from having lunch with Campbell Mitchell-Cotts.[213] I'd reported him a 1st edition of *Dorian Gray* which he'd

213 The brother of a friend of Anne's brother Antony.

said he'd wanted; I bought it for £2. 10/- and reported it for £4. He rang this morning, said he'd have it, and asked me to lunch at the Queen's Restaurant, Sloane Square – he'd pick me up in a taxi. I said yes, and then was appalled and longed to get out of it, especially being so huge, having no hat or jewellery, only dirty utility[214] maternity dress and Sheila's striped smock. However, it wasn't bad. I think he must be queer really. He had another 'protégé' there, a seventeen-year-old Canadian soldier, good-looking and rather nice; blushing desperately nearly all the time with all the ghastly embarrassing things Campbell kept saying. Campbell's joke was to call him 'the baby' all the time, and say things like 'he forgot to take his syrup of figs last night; I had to scold him'; not in the least funny. The other people were his bank manager, very subservient and also embarrassed, and a ghastly fawning boring woman of about 40. They were quite funny to watch when Campbell said things like: 'When Baby came in there was I without clothes on and Mrs Harding sitting on the lavatory.' Campbell wrote a cheque and paid me for the *Dorian Gray* in the middle of lunch, so that was quite good. He talked a great deal about my giving birth, in a way he hoped would embarrass me, but it didn't at all; I was better I thought than I'd ever been with him before. He was going to see Edith Sitwell tomorrow. When I told him about your seeing her he tried to make me come too. But as it was at her ladies' club, she asking him, not he her, though I rather longed to, I thought it would probably be a mistake and only lead to fearful embarrassment, so said I couldn't as I had someone coming to tea.

Writing this at my desk in the window, it is rather nice watching people pass as I write. The white blossomed tree is at its very best today. Nearly everybody stares at it, and quite a lot of people stop to go on looking longer.

Had a day of practically *no* work at all yesterday which was rather awful. Sheila half the morning and for lunch, which I enjoyed. She was very interesting about babies and children; she always is. I said could she possibly come and stay for a night or two once a fortnight, and act as my Welfare Officer.

Then there was a Ruth crisis. Nancy rang up to say that Fidelity had rung up to say that Antony had wired, saying he had leave and

214 Clothing made from cloth which fulfilled certain government requirements and at government fixed prices. (Later, in 1942, utility furniture was introduced.)

Ruth must go (yesterday night) to Glasgow for the weekend. We got hold of Ruth in the end, after great difficulties (she was in London taking the little boys to Liverpool Street). She got very fussed and worried, and at first didn't think it would be possible, because the furniture removers were coming on Monday, and she had all her packing to do, and no clothes.[215] However, in the end, she put off the removers, and I lent her clothes, face-creams, a dress, a mass of things, and off she went.

It's 20 past 5 so I must post this.

Love
ANNE

From ANNE   10 Warwick Avenue
Saturday, 10 April, 8.48 p.m.

Darling Heywood,

Have just come back from the Great Western Hotel. I really must stop going there. My evenings out are a great difficulty; when I am delivered I think I really must try Norway again as a regular thing. Nancy says she has now started saying certain people have the evil eye and bring her bad luck, and turning them out.

On the way back from Paddington, so as to get home as quickly as possible, I sneaked round the back of a mountain of mail bags and up the taxi lane towards Bishop's Bridge. The I heard footsteps behind me and felt certain it was a policeman.[216] I hurried like anything, as I felt if I got a long way up I might be able to persuade him to let me go the rest of the way, by imploring and begging, and promising not to take a taxi. When I was caught up it was by a soldier, who asked me where he could get a bus for Liverpool Street. I told him, and he passed me; then I called out after him that he would do better to take a tube. He said 'Ah. But I don't want to pass through the station, see?' So I said, 'Oh, I *see*.' He said, 'I want to keep clear of the Red Caps,[217] see?' So I said I saw again and laughed, and we talked the rest of the way up the passage; he had a long confused army story about passes and courses and red caps; he was rather nice, cunning and funny.

215 She was about to move from Sheila and John's home near Henley, to Jock and Fidelity's farm at Great Glemham, Suffolk.
216 Pedestrians were not allowed in the taxi lane.
217 Military police.

Francis Watson came here this evening for about half an hour. I am lending him my bicycle. There was some rum for him. He is very nice, I think.

I am having lunch with Jane [Francis Watson's wife] on Monday, Ina on Tuesday. That is all my engagements. I really am saying no if asked out at night now. Ruth probably comes for the night Monday; Mama for weekend on Saturday. Then Monday 19th Ronans.

It is extraordinary how, though I have known really for about 7 months that I should be leaving the shop about now, and have had all that time to prepare, I all the same find myself in a fever of *un*preparedness, and have a *mountain* of things that absolutely *must* be done ahead of me – it's really a bit of a nightmare.

And now on Monday I've got to meet Jo[218] at Paddington at 11.10 and look after her for the day. It is so annoying, as I would so enjoy this if it wasn't for fussing about what I wasn't doing. I like Jo; she amuses me, and I look forward to getting to know her better (and really I know that in fact I shan't fuss while she's there).

I foresee too that what people are going to do for our child is going to be so tremendously much more that we've ever done for theirs, that it will really be rather shaming, and I must stop grumblings over meetings and takings across London etc. (But I wouldn't grumble if I wasn't fussing, on the contrary.)

Sunday afternoon

Am sitting in Regent's Park, which I've walked to for my exercise. It's pleasant, right beside the water; sun occasionally, ducks and swans to watch. The great thing about April is, when it's fine, even you and I can't quite start worrying about the winter coming soon.

Later, 7, home again

Am in the midst of agonies of accounts boredom. Floor, tables, chairs, all covered with statements and invoices.

I achieved writing to Craig today about the lease. It's all a bit terrifying isn't it.

Monday morning, 12th

Your Saturday letter has arrived. I'm very glad you didn't destroy it. You must never do that. I had rather the same melancholy feeling

218 Josephine Hill, Heywood's niece, aged eleven.

while having dinner at the Great Western Hotel on Saturday /- how endlessly much longer must I go on going out to dinners by myself twice a week, and having to read in the evenings night after night here alone? But what luxurious conditions to be melancholy in, compared with yours.

I think it's simply astounding and unimaginable that you or anyone can possibly *ever* recognise these guns and lorries from 1,000s of feet up.

I knew really as I wrote it that I was being rather cruel nagging you about shop questions. You have answered them wonderfully lately, too. I do long to see you. I think we must risk its clashing with the baby if you have a chance of leave soon. We'll talk about it tonight, I hope anyhow

Must now wash, dress, empty po, make bed and meet Jo. (That turns out to be a poem.)

Love

A

From ANNE   10 Warwick Avenue
Tuesday, 13 April

Darling H,

Only time for a short scrap this morning as I couldn't write last night as Ruth came early, and I must must *must* pay bills this morning; I am getting frantic about them.

That nurse is coming, which is rather wonderful; I spoke to her on the telephone. I am very relieved indeed about that.

At the shop Holmden[219] came in (did you know he was the Revd?) and says he'd pay £20 for the Corvo. I said I'd ask you. I think it's rather mean of him really; he said he 'couldn't afford'. But if he can afford £20 he can afford £25.

That Major Jordan wrote back rather excited about the Acker-manns, and very grateful for my trouble. He's coming to see them Friday morning. I do hope it works.

I think that Etty book is going to sell like anything. Nancy is very useful at knowing who to send prospectuses to; I wouldn't have known about Mrs Colin Anderson for instance, who ordered one by return of post. Nancy has already sent 12 prospectuses and only

219 Richard Frank Douglas Holmden, at this time Canon of St Andrew-by-the-Wardrobe, Blackfriars; later Canon of St Alphege.

reached B in the alphabet. I've asked the publishers (F. Lewis) for 70 more. It would be awful if we got a lot of eager orders and then couldn't send them.

I rather *think*, though Nancy does not quite say so, that the Hester dinner was rather a success as far as Hester was concerned – I mean as far as Nancy's idea of H. is concerned. But Nancy is rather proud and won't quite admit. She is giving Hester parmesan cheese, a good sign I think. I am pleased.

Must stop and pay bills. Am meeting Ina for lunch at the Ariston, at 5 to 12. Lovely day, and I feel very lazy.

Love
ANNE

From HEYWOOD   Matlock
                                        Wednesday, 14 April
Darling,

I tried twice to ring you up on Monday night – but all the trunk lines were engaged.

One of the men in this room went on working till 3 a.m. I went on till 12. One's result after hours of struggle is often pathetic. Mine is. I have no doubt now of failure and doom.

One of the young men in the room wants to order *Horizon* for a year. Is that quite impossible now? I've enclosed his address. Couldn't Nancy ring up Cyril [Connolly] and say it's for a soldier? I'd like to get if for him.

I meant not to ask you to do anything this week. It must be desperate for you. You were wonderfully brave going off to lunch with Campbell. Your description made me laugh – I rather long for you to have met Edith and to know what Campbell would say to her.

I am an awful thing called syndicate leader, starting today for 3 days, which means being responsible for everyone's photos and apparatus and things. A lot of extra fret.

I must dust now – I got up early to write this but time has gone. Reade is still a bit snappy and sulky. He's moody like Roger Hinks. It's like *The Magic Mountain*[220] – with the doom hanging over one. I *do* think of you a lot now.

Love
H

220 The novel by Thomas Mann about a TB sanatorium.

[166]

From ANNE

In the shop
Wednesday, 14 April, 11.30

Darling Heywood,

It was very annoying about last night as I was *not* out at all; I can't *think* why they said I was; I think it was silly little Marlene's fault, who said she'd seen me go out; really I was either in the lav, or doing the blackout upstairs. And tonight you'll think I'll be out because of its being the Sternsons' night out; really I shall probably be in eating sandwiches.

I felt very low, depressed, anxious and worried this morning early, but am better again now. Can't succeed in getting much clearing or work done; interruptions abound. Am now trying to screw up my courage to go down and tactfully attempt to sack the Lesters [cleaners at the shop].

Isn't it awful, Mrs Breakwell's[221] son is 'wounded and missing' – Nancy has written to her as from all of us. I think I might too – except I can't think what to say – I wish I could think of something we could actually do for her.

Anne Toynbee has had a girl[222] 3 days ago; I happened to pick up a *Times* someone had left in a bus and saw it.

Must take this to the post now.

All devoted love from
ANNE

PS Have just been down to Mrs Lester. Miraculously (it can't go *on*, this luck we're having – touch wood, Lord have mercy) it was like the Smiths. She is *almost* sure Mr Lester would be only too pleased not to have the work to do.

Evening

I missed the post with this letter as my watch had stopped and it had been much later than I'd thought.

Lord Beaverbrook came in this morning. Spent 17 guineas. Bought the guinea book, *Canadian Scenery*, and an old book, forget its name, about travels in America. He was very showing-off, and bargained too – the amount should have been 19 guineas. It was lucky I was there, as it was a lunch hour, with only Mrs Kentall.

A Mrs Young (who knows you) is hiver-havering over both the Negro and the Picture Clock – doubt if she'll buy either though. Mr

221 Former cleaner in the shop.
222 Josephine Toynbee.

[167]

Lester is getting the clock to work tomorrow, and she's coming in to have another look. I did do a fair amount of filing and clearing today.

Must now eat filthy, disgusting sandwiches. Will be sick I expect.

From HEYWOOD   Matlock
[About Wednesday, 14 April]

Darling Anne,

I am so obsessed with all this and almost mad that I can't do anything but boringly go on about it. With all the excuses I make to myself for not having 'done better', I think I've been very unlucky. If only I sat next to someone who would cooperated, instead of Mackenzie, I think I could have passed. Cooper and Reade work together and tell each other everything – as do nearly all the others. It is maddening and exasperating, because I believe I *could* do it all all right – which I never felt about the stuff at Larkhill.

Have I said I leave here on the 27th and go back to Wentworth (alone with Mackenzie). I believe I could get the last weekend off, as the work will be over then – but I shouldn't get to Ronans till about six or seven on Saturday, and would have to leave probably before lunch on Sunday so I think it's hardly worth it.

I asked about baby leave, and they said that you must have a wire sent after delivery – so you arrange for me to be wherever you'd like best – Windsor or Ronans. It'll probably be about 4 days.

Love

H

From HEYWOOD   [About 15 April 1943]
Darling Anne,

I've done one of our typical things and have lost a half-written anti-Mackenzie letter. It was very venomous – so it will be uncomfortable if he finds it. I did a paper so badly yesterday that there's no more hope of passing – as one has to get a v. high percent. I'm full of chagrin and fury and rage and misery.

I got out for an hour last night – it was lovely – so warm and spring-like.

Brilliant about that nurse. Have you seen her? Do you think you ought to?

Just got your Lester letter. How incredibly lucky, and what an awful lot of interviews you're having to do.

I'm syndicate leader for 3 days, so must start fussing round for a key. I write such scrappy wretched letters.

Love

H

From ANNE [Probably Thursday, 15 April] Morning
Darling Heywood,

I think I shall be able to get *Horizon* for Gus Davies – they accepted a new subscription quite meekly not long ago.

Osbert says that Edith likes Campbell. Isn't it extraordinary? Osbert's in a great deal every day. He continues to be much concerned about you. I love seeing him – he makes me laugh so – but *oh* the difficulties of getting work done (grumble grumble once again).

Evening

I am getting on really fairly well with clearing, at last. Have been all through my notebook with Nancy yesterday and today – Nancy was very nice. It was a most boring sort of thing to be doing (though essential), and she stood it extremely well. Have paid every bill that has come in right up to date, which has made us rather overdrawn. But I don't think it matters, as very little will have to be paid out now for a long time, and Mollie will be going on sending bills, and as she does them quicker than me the money will come in sooner. She will be gradually adding up the day books too – I shall be interested to know about that. It hasn't been done since October. I long to know about Christmas. It seemed to be very good, but it's so hard to tell.

Nancy has been altogether very nice lately, as well as funny as always. She gives me an impression (touching wood a million times) of being more 'settled' than I've ever thought her before.

I'm going to make a great effort to be in the shop early tomorrow when Major Jordan arrives. *Do* hope he buys the things.

A serious thing is I have lost the notebook with the list of all the things to remind myself to do, and that is very serious indeed.

It makes *all* the difference that I shall have a monthly nurse here. Otherwise I should have to think of every detail for the baby today and tomorrow, and should be in a fearful fuss. Now I needn't bother at once about finding a woman to wash nappies, or about Ross going to a nursery school; it can all wait till I come back, and Mrs Sternson may be able to find out while I am away. I think I shall have the nurse for 3 weeks, unless she's an absolute demon.

I am getting really vast now, quite frightening to look at. People invariably get up for me in buses which is rather splendid and in Regent's Park on Sunday some youths called after me 'Not long to wait now.'

A wonderful thing has happened to make Nancy polite to Americans. She has been told that there is an American private soldier (rather like that sergeant that everybody knows [Stuart Preston]) called Aggie Duke, who lives at the Dorchester and has £2,000,000 (not dollars). And as it is difficult to tell the difference between American officers and men, it has quite transformed her behaviour to them all. One came in (she said) at 6 the other day, and instead of hustling him out, she hung about for half an hour while he wandered round. She had an intuition that he *was* Aggie Duke, and she still thinks he might have been.

Ruth is here today, poised between 2 lives. It was very nice seeing her alone, which I hadn't for a long time. We had a drink with Angela [Culme-Seymour], and the negro conductor was there; he's called Rudolph. He *was* very nice as I'd thought. If you had been there we might have asked him to come and listen to our gramophone records. (Except there are no needles, you'd have never let that happen.)

It's a waste for the baby to be still in the womb in this wonderful weather.

Jim McKillop is on embarkation leave – isn't it awful? He's coming to the shop this afternoon. I'm not going to be there.

I am writing this in bed. This morning angelic Mrs Sternson offered to give me breakfast in bed every day till I go – I said Yes – it is very nice. Must get up now though.

Love

A

From HEYWOOD   Matlock
                                                       Saturday, 17 April
Today Mackenzie actually made a sort of apology. Said he felt

'mean' not telling me things, but he thought of it all as a 'competition' (which it isn't) and he wanted to send in an individual paper.

Today we've been given the programme for next week. It's a sort of crisis programme. Exercises lasting for the whole day, and work and lectures in the evening – so I may not write. I think we're told the results in the afternoon before we go. That's Tuesday week.

Astounding weather. I didn't get out yesterday, but did for a bit on Friday. Cooper and Reade and I often go to a little pub on the hill and drink beer – we shan't be able to next week. There's a sort of terraced garden in front of the Hydro with tennis courts and lawns – I'm there now. It's wonderful really this place – compared with where I have been or probably ever will be. Like a bearable school – with all the sort of school undercurrents going on. Reade has thawed again and is amusing. We call Mackenzie 'red blood' because when I raged about him R. perversely said he didn't agree. He was 'full of red blood'. He's not at all. His face is pitted and Reade thinks he must have had syphilis in Morocco. Then there's a man we call 'Gimlet'. He's in their room and makes a noise like a gimlet in his sleep. A sort of ginger-moustached beer drinker who's about as fogged as I am – quite jolly. Of the other two in my room Jameson is 'ordinary' and rather a bore, Drewe has a better mind and would be bearable alone. They are boring together, making facetious jokes all the time. There's one called Franklin in C. & R.'s room – an ex-bank clerk with a bald head who's tremendously on their nerves, with a soft little precise voice that goes on and on. He is always dusting their room and telling them the time is 24½ minutes past. Reade says rude things about him much too loud.

Albert has arrived from Wentworth in the process of his course. They do two weeks here. I haven't spoken to him properly yet.

How awful about Mrs Breakwell's son – I do feel sorry. Is there much shop money still to come in? If we're overdrawn I think we ought to go slow on buying. Harry might easily ask for his credit too. Did Craig ever answer about the lease?

Perhaps I ought to write to Nancy about the buying?

Percival[223] came down to talk to the class yesterday. It was like God coming. Even all the officers stood up. It was all rather frightening. 'When we start our big show' and all that.

223 Major Percival, an important figure in Photographic Interpretation.

This is the nicest part of the week – with Monday still quite far off.

There's no hope of next weekend now. No travel at Easter. I didn't know it was Easter. They've arranged a lecture so that people shan't catch the train. I wish I could have seen you at your most enormous. Make Charles [Lambe] do one of his huge enlargements.

Love

H

From FRANCES PARTRIDGE   Ham Spray House
                                          Marlborough
                                          Sunday, 18 April

My dear Heywood,

I was delighted to get your mummified postcard. Is that what you are feeling like? Or what you long for, in a far too energetic existence? I should think a hydro must be an improvement on your last lodgings, but how dreadful for you to have all this fidgety brainwork, and in the *heat*! I feel as if I could never do such a thing again – as brainwork I mean. In fact the effort of struggling through Gerald's new book on Spain[224] is a good deal too severe for me, and I fear that (greatly humiliated) I shall have to toss it aside unfinished.

It is really grisly the way everyone has been scattered far and wide – will you ever be moved south to a more accessible region, and will you get compassionate leave for the arrival of your child? I'm afraid my attempt to get you a beautiful starched French nanny with black boot-button eyes was useless – she had already been snapped up. I wonder if Anne has secured one yet. I have not alas seen her, we haven't budged to London for weeks, not since R.'s tribunal, when I thought her looking very well indeed. That Nancy of yours frightened me rather. R.'s appeal went off gloriously, with bows and beaming smiles on all sides – a great relief. And then one regretted all the days of worry and running over unnecessary arguments beforehand.

Since then illness has separated us from our only neighbours. I got a delightful little bout of 'flu, very harmless and restful – and then Julia [Strachey] got it – very badly and had a temperature of

224 Gerald Brenan's *The Spanish Labyrinth*.

102 and 103 for a week. Laurence nursed her most devotedly, but came bicycling round now and again in a slight frenzy. He described her as 'lying as flat as anything' with a bandage over her eyes, and insisting on the temperature being taken 5 times a day. We were rather worried about her, as she seemed to have called in a sort of military horse doctor, who didn't sound much use, and muttered about pneumonia, but in the end pleurisy was what it was called. She has been ill I think for some time, but still rejects all my offers of reading aloud etc. and persists in lying doggo.

We now have Isobel [Strachey] staying, who looks as fresh as a daisy and has as usual the most wonderful stories of pick-ups. She became inflamed by the idea of being taken to the Savoy by Americans, and when she heard a Yankee voice in the darkness telling someone the way, she shrieked out 'An American!' – 'Were you looking for one?' asked Major Foley, and took her back to his room at Mount Royal, where he had a bottle of whisky (96% alcohol). One sip and the room started going round and round. Then the major told her strings of anecdotes, each ending in 'See?' and then there was a rough and tumble on the bed – after which she discovered to her horror that he was a 'priest' – I suppose she means an army chaplain.

We haven't otherwise any gossip. I'm afraid there is no news of Rollo – I'm trying to get an enquiry sent to the Vatican, but somehow feel he is dead and I think Janetta does too.[225] Bunny and Angelica are having a baby.[226] Babies are in the air all right – Isobel has been describing Jennifer Fry's,[227] which is a Bright Young Person already – exquisitely beautiful with huge dark eyes and hundreds of young titled godparents.

We have just booked rooms in Mrs Cornish's farm which you gave the address of at Welcomb. I can't remember what you told us about it – but she actually seemed quite eager to have us.

Have you any idea yet what your future is going to be like? If you have time I would love to hear some news of you – and what your existence is like – I take a morbid interest in the details of military life. I hope you are writing down your experiences.

225 He was, but the first Janetta knew officially was when his clothes arrived back in a parcel.
226 David Garnett and his second wife Angelica. Angelica was pregnant with Amaryllis.
227 Victoria Heber-Percy. Daughter of Jennifer Ross and Robert Heber-Percy.

If I can collect any gossip I will write again – we have just been through a singularly arid period and now this blazing sun drives everything from my head.

Much love meanwhile from us both.

Yours

FRANCES

From ANNE   Ronans

Tuesday morning, 20 April (still in bed)

Darling Heywood,

Incredibly, it is a wonderful morning again, after pouring with rain and getting really quite cold yesterday.

It gives me a peculiar feeling being here. Rather flat, melancholy and anxious (not about anything special). Not the delightful holiday-escape feeling I was expecting. It was nice, though, at Warwick Avenue having Mary to pack, and is nice having her here, as it stops one having to worry over the extra work one is causing.

At night now I begin to keep thinking and dreaming that the baby is starting; though it's very unlikely, as it's not due for nearly a fortnight, and I am sure, really, it will be late. The doctor says if it hasn't come by Sunday week. I must go up to London to see him on the Monday after – I've had to make an appointment. I'm rather appalled. He says that will probably start it, and someone must accompany me. He says it would be much better if it was *possible* for you not to come till 3 or 4 days after it's born, as I shall be rather weak, exhausted and sleepy the first few days, and it would be a waste. So I thought, supposing it was born the 2nd, Ma might send you a wire saying it was, and add: 'Could you possibly come 6th' and you could show the wire to your CO (or whoever it would be). I think, when you get to Wentworth next week, if possible you'd better wire your new address – or you may know it in advance. As we ought to know where you are. Also, I'd rather like a wire if you pass the exam, as I long to hear.

Am now out in the garden (11 a.m.), in a thin silk maternity dress kindly lent me by Angela. It *is* very pleasant here indeed, cuckoo cuckooing and everything looking so pretty. Peta has migraine every day at certain hours, and doesn't look very well. It does worry me what a bore our being here really must be for her. Though she was very welcoming and *behaves* as if it wasn't.

[174]

Ma is sleeping badly. I seem to be the healthiest (the doctor yesterday said again about the baby being in an excellent position, and that he anticipated no difficulties).

The aeroplanes are deafening and don't stop for a moment, which is the disadvantage of this place.

There's a tiresome letter from your bank which would be almost impossible to answer even if we were both at home – asking for dividend counterfoils and tax certificates, pass books and statement sheets, and dozens of other things we shall never be able to find. I shall write to them saying I can't answer for 6 weeks. Or six months.

Will now stop and write various other letters.

Fondest love from
ANNE

From HEYWOOD Matlock
Thursday, 22 April

Darling,

We went flying yesterday afternoon – which was a great relief – to be able to stop working. It was a lovely day, and we went for an hour in a charabanc down Dovedale. All glades and streams. But the spring this year seems out of the window. I mean it goes on, surprisingly and beautifully, but life is too dreary to be able to enjoy it much. I had a wonderful Frances letter (I'll send it if I find it). She said they'd just had a 'very arid' period.

We 'went up' about 6 at a time for 3 hours, to look at the ground and compare it with a photograph. It was like a Marx Brothers film. Cooper had to keep winding some handle, and the aeroplane kept suddenly dropping when we all bowed down together, and we all got tangled up in wrongly fixed parachutes. A good many hadn't flown before and were nervous. I went deaf as usual, and got caught up in the parachute getting out.

Otherwise it's just been slaving away. It's getting more and more school-like. A great deal of drawing, and my little sketches etc. are always so miserable. It's now quite 100 to 1 against me – so don't expect a telegram. It's a terrible psychological moment for you for me to fail isn't it? *Poor* Harriet.

I can imagine the sort of slump feeling you describe on getting to Ronans.

I think my address at Wentworth will be 3rd Company, Intelligence Corps Depot, Nr Rotherham. What will yours be?

Love my dear – it must be horribly agitating for you – all the waiting and wondering about Harriet.

H

From NANCY MITFORD

[Postmark 22 April (Thursday)]

Anne you [are] naughty – Mollie remembers Mr Swann[228] leaving the list, and it's no good making excuses to him, as the list is for books for my brother-in-law [Oswald Mosley] in prison, and we can't get another. It happened when I was at Sotheby's that day. Do try and think, Mollie says she thought afterwards you hadn't given it to me. I really feel in despair, it is so unkind to him, and he'll never understand – Swann said he even came back again and said 'Will you be *sure* to give it to her.'

No I didn't understand about Julia [Strachey] and sent the books to her. I thought they were for her young lover you see. Oh Bugger.

Desperately busy – £30 yesterday in trifles nothing over £1, so you can imagine . . .

I feel slightly overwhelmed, and can't find these blasted Ouida things either.

I dare say by Monday I shall feel calmer.

Is *Voice and Verse* (OUP) for you?

A quieter moment and I feel less fussed. Please how much is the clock picture?

Your Stern man doesn't like it (engraving).

Another £20 today – quite like Xmas rush.

Love from
NM

PS I see this letter sounds highly hysterical but don't take much notice, only if you *could* remember where you put poor Mr Swann's list –? [Anne remembers nothing whatever about this episode.]

228 Michael Swann, author/explorer, who wrote a fine travel book about going up the Orinoco.

From HEYWOOD   Matlock
                                    [postmark Friday, 23 April]
Darling,

I've utterly abandoned hope of passing today. I've found out that
I made a complete mess of the exercise we had to do, and it's full of
hideous mistakes; I've got back all the dumb dud feelings I used to
have at Eton.

The consolations are that it's been five weeks off from drill and
tweeny work, and that there's only one more full day of this sort of
torture, and then 3 days of relax before the other sort begins again.
Reade is going to Wentworth too which is nice – but not Cooper.
He's going to Leeds.

I haven't heard a cuckoo here yet.

                                                            Later
I began to do some work, when R. and C. came to collect me, so I
went out with them and got into a nice don't-care state. We went to
a pub and drank, and put dominoes up on end so that they fell
down, and then went to the Methodist Church (which is the only
possible canteen – where you get halfpenny sandwiches. We call
them 'dust' as it's like eating dust). The ping-pong goes on, and the
parson wanders round chatting with the men. I don't know why we
don't all get scurvy. I never have salad or fruit not – and hardly any
green veg. but live on endless cakes and buns. Little boils do begin.
Everyone is v. frightened of the exercise, which is starting in 10
minutes. It's called Exercises Various, and they fear it's some dreadful isolated test.

Oh Lord!

I met Albert in the passage and he said he's now engaged to
Monica.

                                                              H

From HEYWOOD   Matlock
                                                    Friday, 24 April
Darling,

Worse and worse. We had a rush exercise all yesterday morning. Different photos were given, and we had to identify, and then
they were snatched away and a new lot given. And I took the
scale wrong – all my blasted aeroplanes turned out enormous and
wrong. I told Major Moles what I'd done and he said 'Ah – but

that's what you might do on operations.' So I'm a total wreck – sunk and foundered. It's the general opinion that Major Moles is the boss. He's a rather nice dry man – impeccable with frightening knowledge. Anyhow, nothing more can be done now – and there's no homework to do any more. On Tuesday, at 3 o'clock, I'll have to go in to be sacked. Cooper is a bit better than me and might scrape through. Reade certainly will. But I'm afraid Mackenzie will too. He can draw beautiful maps..

It's sometimes fascinating gazing through the stereoscope at those photos, and looking down deep ravines and over cliffs. But there's not time to wander about among them. You must concentrate on a tiny little thing which might be a hideous tank or which might be a native latrine. It often becomes exasperating, and my eyes swim. In the dark now in bed, little specks float together in my eyes. I'm nauseated by war weapons – photos of them on all the walls – photos through the stereo – slides – films. I look at much of *Picture Post* with feeling of work and disgust because of them.

Those who pass and those who fail all go back to their units. And my unit seems to be Wentworth. There they'll make us drill and dust and do PT till they think of something else. Here the ones who pass will be posted to one of the photo places after a week or two. I suppose I shall moulder on at Wentworth until they think of somewhere else to send me to by mistake.

R. and C. and I are going to Buxton by bus in about 10 minutes time. It's the only place we can think of going to. It's of course cold, and all the shops will be shut. How I wish I was flying to you.

The Orchards[229] say they want to see me and to have lunch in London – either to or fro.

A great bore about Wentworth is that it's almost impossible to telephone from.

It's awful being both physically and mentally so incapable. I've decided that all I can do is to decide whether a novel is good or bad. It's time to go to Buxton. I think of you in the drawing-room at Ronans.

Love as ever

H

229 See Appendix.

Monday, 26 April

Darling,

I will send this to Wentworth Woodhouse. It will be dreadful for you to be back there again I fear, and to be bustled and jostled and have to carry buckets of pee again, and all the rest. But better that Reade is going too.

There is nothing whatsoever to say from here somehow. Day after day is so exactly identical. I am afraid Peta must surely be longing for us to go. It is dreadful that it may quite easily be another 3 weeks.

Ma and I go for long walks, stumble about in the woods and get lost and covered with blood.

Would you like any food sent to you at WW? Is Mrs S. sending the washing all right? Don't forget to send her your new address. Shall long to hear the WW news.

Love
A

I do dislike writing to you at Wentworth Woodhouse, as for one thing if it's like the last time you won't get this letter for at least 6 weeks, or more probably never.

From HEYWOOD   Matlock
Monday, 26 April, 10.45 a.m.

Darling,

I couldn't ring up on Saturday night because didn't get in till after 10. We went to Buxton, which is a quarter of an hour in the bus and got there at 1.30. Then started the usual hunt for food, being refused at one hotel after another. We had a pink gin after that, and it became quite funny. We were at last allowed into a café and given a piece of spam. There is a nice bit of the town with an eighteenth-century crescent and a rotunda. I went into some antique shops, but found nothing except a sewing case made into a book. No books. Then we wandered rather desultorily. Reade was in a mood. Tea in a dusty winter garden. One does so much sitting, and fighting ennui and a feeling of the constant waste of time. At 6 we began to drink again, and that was fun. Then back in the bus, very pretty drive down a dale, all the spring whizzing by.

There is a rumour, which sounds true, that six people have

failed. Everyone is in a gloomy fever. In my room they keep weighing up and considering each person. I think I am more resigned than most, because I expect to fail, but am gloomy at leaving here, and leaving Cooper, who has been a huge bolster.

I shall probably have to spend a night at Warwick Av, on the way to Windsor, as my train won't get in till about 8, and I couldn't get to you in time to see you that night. And I shall have to go to W. Av to get clothes.

The course that Albert is on is also going back to WW tomorrow – which is a bore because we'll have to march to the station with them instead of on our own – and go in the train with them. Mackenzie and Reade and Harris and I are going. Reade is having to leave at once – is already due in London.

Yesterday we were sent out to find our way across country from photos. We were split up. I was with Mackenzie and Jameson. Mackenzie was tiresome, and told me I was holding the photo wrong, and that I'd rub off the marks of where we were to go. It wasn't too bad at all. A terrific gale and we were in lonely moors like *Withering Heights*.

I've seen *Desert Victory*, *War in the West*, *The Vasgso Raid*, *the Battle of Crete*, and many many more.

If you haven't had a telegram by the time you get this, you'll know my failure is sure. I shan't be able to write tomorrow because of the move.

Love, my dear. Beastly this cold weather for you, and making long long days.

H

Ronans
Wednesday, 28 April

Darlingest Heywood,

Two lovely long letters from you today. Am longing now to hear from WW, about your last interview, and about what WW is like this time. I fear it can't not be simply awful being back there again. If only this wretched baby would start now, it would obviously be the most convenient possible time and you might even get a week I should think. But it is sure to wait until you are started on some new course which will be impossible to leave.

Try to arrange to have your Orchard lunch and shop time on your way *to* and not from me, as the later you arrive and the later you can stay with me the better.

Nice hot sunny day today, which makes all the difference. Mama and I go on longer and longer walks, and more and more scrambling and difficult. I fall into ditches, and trip over brambles etc; it must be most uncomfortable for Harriet but doesn't make her come out. Tomorrow we're going for a joggly bus ride and exhausting shop in Bracknell – perhaps that may do something. The worst of it is that it's not yet even due.

It has been rather nice up to yesterday thinking the shop was safely shut for Easter. Nancy writes rather flustered-sounding letters – *not* reassuring – I'll keep a sample or two to show you. She says there's a great boom on, and she's been selling £20 to £30 a day. So the work must be being pretty desperate with the 2 of them only – except that Mrs K. will be doing more and more. And it won't be for very long.

Fondest dearest love from

ANNE

I've just had a letter from some auctioneers, saying we've got £7. 7/- for that old sofa Aunty Coy[230] gave us. Rather splendid isn't it?

The baby was now very nearly due – on 2 May. Anne's letters have so far been mostly about the shop and her day-to-day life and, except occasionally, not a great deal emerges from them about her attitude to pregnancy, the birth and the baby. Nor is much more to be learnt from those she wrote after the baby was born, partly because Heywood had four days' leave then, and partly because several letters are missing from the following weeks.

Meanwhile Heywood's army life continued its roller-coaster progress. He rang up from Wentworth Woodhouse on the evening of 28 April. Before leaving Matlock he had been given the news that he had failed the exam. Anne had been out walking with her mother when he rang, and Peta Lambe took the message.

---

230 Constance Jarvis. Her maiden name had been Hunter Blair; she was Anne's mother's aunt, and Ralph Jarvis's mother.

From ANNE   Ronans
                    Wednesday, 28 April. Evening in bed
Darling Heywood,

Too sad about the bad news, after all the sweat and trouble. And having been to some extent interested for the first time makes it sadder. And now the waiting about for an interview again. Oh dear.

I am generally out walking with Ma between tea and dinner. Is that your best telephoning time? If so, say, and I could alter our day's programme.

Did you get the £3 all right?

Everything's all right here. I begin to wonder if the baby is coming soon, as I notice one or two symptoms – sort of cramps in my bottom, and Harriet heaving about particularly violently.

Fondest love
ANNE

6

Wentworth Woodhouse and the Birth of the Baby

From HEYWOOD   14335674
Wentworth Woodhouse
Thursday, 29th

Darling Anne,

Reade and I are sitting in the lavatory because we can't find the place where we're supposed to go to next, and we can't go to the barrack room because that's not allowed. We've just stood in a queue for 1½ hours for our pay, wearing gas masks for half an hour of the time.

This morning I had to separate the paper from the dust in the bins, and then rake some earth under a tree where nothing could possibly grow. Reade and I are in a Nissen hut. All the others are horrid. Sort of ex-Stock-Exchange clerks, who in the Army become dreadful.

As usual there's nowhere to put anything in. It's lowering indeed to come back here, and the feeling of Reade going off early next week, and of my quite likely getting put into the next course here, or else going back to Larkhill, makes it all worse. But it may get better after a day or two. I suppose I'll be interviewed soon.

I felt after I'd telephoned last night that the message I gave to Peta was full of rather dreadful things to ask you to do – but after I'd arrived and sat in the barrack room and moped (a man learning to play the saxophone being a last straw), I thought I *must* ring you up. The telephone in the village was broken, so I made poor Reade walk all the 3 miles to the station (where we'd had to march from in the afternoon), and then I took hours to get through. Then speaking to Peta it became all dreadful messages. I did – *first* my dear – want to know how you are.

It was rather awful hearing about my failure even though I so expected it. The man was nice. Said he was sorry, but he wasn't allowed to recommend 'borderline' cases from 'other ranks'.

I then asked if he couldn't find me some humble job connected with it in some way, and he did say he'd see what he could do.

I don't know if he will or what it would be – uncommissioned of course.

Reade and Cooper passed. Mackenzie failed. R. & C. were v. sympathetic, and said that they were sure I'd have passed if I'd been in their syndicate, and that they always used to copy half of the other's answers, and could never have done it all by themselves.

I had of course a sneaking delight in Mackenzie's failure – but it's really a great bore as he'll now go on being here and I'll be in perpetual contact with him.

The major – when he told Cooper he'd passed – asked if he'd mind going abroad. He did say 'You're not married are you?' Reade will probably go to GHQ London. Percival, when he came down, said, 'Many of you will be wanted for overseas service.' Also I think it probably is v. bad for eyes. People say so. But I wish I had passed. The sort of chivvied tweeny life here among nobody one likes is difficult to keep sane in.

It was sad parting from Cooper.

I couldn't be writing you a gloomier letter could I? Just when I should be sending you a real soother. Is it awful suspense for you waiting – or do you just feel impatient?

I got your letter this morning. The mail is terribly badly arranged here. One has to dig it out and one never knows when. Will you thank Mama v. much for the letter. Will you tell her when she wires to put her name. It won't be long before I see you now my dear. Even if it is 3 weeks.

> All my love
>
> H

From ANNE   Ronans
                                                Friday, 30 April
Darling Heywood,

I'm getting rather neurotic, and spent about 2 hours awake last night trying to decide whether I was having pains or not. But soon they will turn out to be real, and the house will be roused, and there will be bustle and commotion, packing and telephoning, all on account of me, and I'll be hustled off with Mr Gough – great drama. I wish you were here for it.

Shopped in Bracknell yesterday – got very successful presents for Andrew[231] who spends all day lowering things with string from windows and pulling them up again. So Mama got him a hank of rope and I gave him a pulley, and now he can haul really big things up and down from the ground on to trees etc; he is gratifyingly delighted.

Fondest love
ANNE

From ANNE   Ronans
Saturday, 1 May (morning in bed)

Darling Heywood,

Got your Wentworth letter this morning. How wonderful that Mackenzie failed too; that is very good news. I long to hear what will have happened at your interview – can't quite make out whether that will be yesterday or today.

Lovely day, must get up soon. Charles [Lambe] is here – he is always very genial and jovial these days, and also cheering about the war. He says for instance that the Germans will all be out of Tunisia by the latest in 3 weeks. Joyce Gascoigne's husband is in this Tunisian fighting (as a general) – in one battle his regiment lost 600 out of 2,000 men. Charles always knows just where he is: last weekend he was about 15 miles behind the fighting, this w.e. he is actually in it. However Charles has told Joyce that he is still not fighting.

Be careful of this *Horizon* won't you – have you still got the others? I will enclose a Julia letter if I can find it – *do* send me your Frances. Julia has been having pneumonia.

I find curiously that as my time grows nearer I am less and less apprehensive. And I increasingly *long* to be in the nursing home with the baby born and visible. Each night I feel, if *only* it could start tonight it will probably with luck be over by teatime tomorrow; I shall have seen the baby, know about whether it's boy or girl, telegrams will have been sent, you'll be coming, etc. etc.

231 Andrew Mylius, then aged nine, Peta's son by her first husband Victor (Bobby) Mylius.

It is rather agonising I must say to think of Reade at GHQ in London, and you where you are.

All love, I *hope* I shall see you this week.

A

From ANNE   Ronans
        Sunday, 2 May [the day the baby was due] 10.30 p.m., in bed
Darling H,

Glad you are getting my letters all right this time. I still go on trying to get khaki socks for you, but they seem quite impossible wherever I am. What is your size called? I now have to try and choose by comparing with my own feet.

I am annoyed at having to go to London tomorrow. I find I don't really want to go to the shop at all. It has at last got to seem so delightfully remote, because I feel there is nothing I can do about anything now. But I know that going there tomorrow will make it all real again temporarily, which I don't want, and worrying. This last fortnight has been a wonderful rest and escape, and I am very glad I came and didn't stay in London.

Do go on grumbling and complaining, as I like, want to, *must*, know. And you needn't worry about worrying me, as my present situation is such a sort of protective blanket that I can't really worry, so long as you are not sent abroad. If that happened I should simply die.

From HEYWOOD   Wentworth Woodhouse
                                                          Sunday, 2 May
Darling,

I'll tell you what I've done today. Reade and I were on cookhouse fatigues. It was lucky it was Reade. We had to carry bins to the salvage dump, and put it all through sieves, and separate paper and dust and glass and old food. There were some bad high fish which we had to dig a pit for and bury. Then sweep the yard. Then the floor of the cookhouse. Appalling stench. An ATS sergeant lost her temper and began flinging indiscriminate pails of water at us which we had to dodge. Walking across the yard with a pail we walked between a sergeant and the squad he was drilling. There was a roar: 'Come here, you two men!' Then we were exploded but not put on a charge. Then we had to scrape filth off the outside of boilers. Luckily it is shower-bath day. A bus takes us to a colliery and we use their shower baths. That's rather nice – all among the miners.

I enjoy Reade here very much. He gets so angry with everything. On PT there was a thing called 'O'Grady on parade'. You only obey commands when the Corporal prefixes 'O'Grady says ... ' When you get caught you're put in the awkward squad. That made Reade furious. We were both of course caught. General Montgomery's nephew is here. When officers hear the name Montgomery they say, 'Any relation to the general?' And he says, 'Yes, nephew,' – and it's wonderful for them.

It's Saturday now and no signs of interview yet. It probably now won't be before Tuesday.

We're not allowed to till 7 – and when we are there's nowhere much to go, and one is too tired to walk.

I got the money all right – and a letter from you today. I so love hearing from you so often.

Love darling Anne,
HEYWOOD

From HEYWOOD   Wentworth Woodhouse
                                             Monday 3 May
Darling,

I've had the interview. The man was nice, but he said there was no alternative between staying here, going to an OCTU, or back to the RA. He sees me again after this course. It's a beastly course, and I'll hate it – but it's better than going back to Larkhill and after six weeks the worst of it ought to be over. The new unit comes in this Wednesday – so I'll probably have to start then, and they probably won't allow me more than two days' leave. I suppose I must try not to fail this course too.

I was told that why this place is unpleasant is because the boss was afraid of the Intelligence Corps being cissy, so called in a lot of Guards to run it.

The interview was supposed to be at 9, but I wasn't seen till 3, and I've spent a good deal of the time sitting in a bush behind the latrine.

Yesterday I made another dash to Renishaw and took Reade. We were only able to be there 1½ hours as the taxi had broken down. I couldn't resist showing off Osbert and Renishaw to Reade. I think it was all right, though Reade was very silent and nearly rude. It wasn't long enough of course and it wasn't drink time to help us. Edith was in bed with a headache.

Mackenzie was being interviewed after me. I imagine the same thing will happen to him. I spent a good deal of time in the bushes with him. He was inquisitive. Wanted to see a photo of you, asked if I spent 'more time in conversation or in bed', what I used to do with my spare time, and he wondered why I was 'so unsociable' – because I didn't look an 'unsociable type'. He said that he was and looked a 'brutal type'. That he had once had an income of £2,000 a year, but bought property and lost it. With all this he's a bore and I'd like him to go away.

Albert said 'Oh, I know him. He's like a great big girl.' He (Mackenzie) also said he was only interested in art and sex.

Reade and I went for a v. nice walk in the park. To an eighteenth-century obelisk – the tomb of Rockingham; rhododendrons out and bluebells – so much peace near so much strife. We were discovered by a gamekeeper with a gun, who said we weren't allowed in any of the wood, and he ought to take our names and numbers.[232]

Albert came and sat with R. and me in the YMCA one night. Afterwards R. said, 'What a charming simple person.'

I shall feel suicidal if they don't let me come to see you. It's best to tell you that they might not, so that you expect the worst. I'd get leave after 8 weeks here. It is all hell, but it will end, and I'm screwing myself up to be 'plucky'.

Lovely to get two letters from you today, and *Horizon*. I've been able to read in little snatches, and probably will have quite a lot of time during motorbiking, and when R. goes, which will be any day now.

Father will be furious I didn't go to an OCTU. But even suppose I did pass it – I'd only be an ordinary infantry or gunner officer, and

232 Brian Reade wrote to Anne on 26 October 1985 in answer to a letter from her: 'I first met Heywood in about 1938 when he came to sell some eighteenth-century coloured architectural prints to the V&A. I found him next when we both arrived at the Intelligence Corps training depot at Wentworth Woodhouse. A peak of rapport was reached as we sat in the park there one afternoon beneath a statue of Rockingham, when suddenly a gamekeeper appeared. The mere sight of him brought back to us a kind of reality we both abominated.'

there's more chance here of getting some freak job in the end. Of course I'll very likely fail this too.

I'm thinking about you very much.

Love

H

From HEYWOOD   Wentworth Woodhouse
                                                Tuesday, 4 May

Darling,

I'm in the wood behind the latrine once more. I've just come off 'sanitary' fatigues, which meant I had to clean and empty lavatories, and help to empty cess pits. I had to carry a dustbin full of cess, and a lot of it slopped over on to me, so that now I stink. You'd better burn this letter in case it carries some frightful germs, which you might give to Harriet. I got off at 3, which is why I must hide till 4.30. Once I start the programme – I suppose on Thursday – there'll be no more of this hiding.

It's a lovely day. I've become surrounded by bluebottles, I suppose because of the cess. Motor bikes roar and sergeants yell. Reade and Harris are angry not to have got away yet. I hate hearing them discuss getting away. I find it hard not to mope. But the course will be too hard and agitating to leave much moping time. After the biking comes stuffing into one's head and learning by heart about the organisation of the German Army – mixed with map reading, PT, and running round the assault course – which is a devilish sort of obstacle race, with greasy poles over pools and ropes to swing over. There's an exam at the end of course.

I believe that even if Harriet had arrived, and I'd got the telegram, I shouldn't have got away yet. They've been so busy interviewing all the people who are leaving here. I shall make a very big effort to make them let me come – if it's only for a night.

Daddy is beginning to talk about Uncle Robert again, but I feel convinced that he can do nothing – unless an OCTU which, unless there was a specialised motive, I don't want. I think that probably, unless one is very lucky, one thing is as bad as another.

Reade is full of contradictions (we're still getting on very well). He complains of articles about what he calls 'little Jack Horners' in the Army – misfits like the ones that come out in *New Writing* – but he is very Jack Hornerish himself. He loathes this place and is bitter about it, but I suspect that he may tell some people afterwards that he enjoyed it. He has been through the course here, and is sadistic about telling me the horrifying things which will happen. At the same time he is sympathetic.

Love

H

From HEYWOOD

Wentworth Woodhouse
Thursday, 6 May

Darling Anne,

Since ringing you up last night, I've been moved down to 2 Company (it's v. important to put that on the address – and not 3 which I've just left).

The course starts tomorrow. I now begin to think that – as I wasn't seen by the officer about leave – I'd better not try to come for about two weeks. Otherwise all the new people who'll be starting with me will have got ahead, and also I shan't have got to know them all. I shan't get more than about 2 nights I think.

I've now of course been separated from Reade. All meals and things for 2 Coy are at different times. But in a way it's a relief to get away from all the people who are soon going to move out, and were always discussing it, and to be among new boys.

I've move all my things three times today before anchoring in the stables themselves once more.

I've also been for a 3-mile cross-country run. I'm writing this on my bunk, and new arrivals keep dribbling in all the time. Fairly tough they look. I shall be able to tell them about the place, which will be nice.

I *will* get to see you.

Love

H

From ANNE

Ronans
Friday, 7 May, in bed in the early morning

Darling H,

I do enjoy your letters, with the descriptions of Reade etc. It is dreadful the thought of the agitations and worries of your dreadful course. What a ghastly ghastly life.

[190]

Everything continues identically here. Walked to Bracknell yesterday with Mama. There's a very pretty way though a wood, past a huge deserted country house, and a deserted Nissen hut encampment, lane, farms etc. Bought a lot of baby clothes at a special famous shop in Bracknell. Came back by bus.

Today looks from bed the best sunniest day we've had for a long time, so I must get up. I am loving it here. I have been thinking, probably never again (or anyhow not for 2 or 3 years at least), shall I have absolutely *nothing* to do like here now, and breakfast in bed, which I do *love*, day after day after day after day.

Andrew [Mylius] in London locked himself in the lavatory and cried for 2 hours over going back to school, refused to and said he wouldn't, and yet he had to. Do let us really be unlike other parents and *not* send our child to boarding school even if it's a boy (*certainly* not if it's a girl).

Devotedest love from

ANNE

Your letters to me seem to take 2 days, not very bad I suppose really. How long do mine?

From HEYWOOD   Wentworth Woodhouse
                                                    Friday, 7 May
Darling,

I'm thoroughly enmeshed again, and everything's a wild rush. I've begun the biking. It's fairly fiendish – like being given some ghastly uncontrollable horse. The instructors bark and scream, there's a great roar of engines, and we wear crash helmets (which are uncomfortable). I haven't fallen off yet, but was sent to the bottom squad as being poor (which is a good thing I think). The engine keeps stopping and then the whole thing crashes to the ground and one has to heave it up. But it's a good thing to get it over in the first 3 weeks. I shall quite likely keep up my splendid record of failures – but it isn't the end, I believe, if one fails in biking.

Then, when one gets in exhausted at 5 after tea, there's a 'shining period' from 6 to 7. Reade hasn't gone yet but I can hardly see him. He got me your letter today – which went of course to 3 Company.

It is quite unbearable the thought of not seeing you for so long (though I *shall* come anyhow for a night).

All my love – I long to see you. Perhaps next weekend – or the one after – I'll be coming.

H

From ANNE   Ronans

Sunday, 9 May

From ANNE

Darling Heywood,

It really is getting rather awful this baby *never* coming. It is a week late now; and tomorrow I shall have been here 3 weeks. I wonder if Peta is getting very sick of us. I think she must be. I would be at *anyone* staying as long as we have.

It's again a filthy, fearfully windy cold cloudy day, it's half past 11 and I am still in bed. I wonder what you are doing, and if you've found any nice new boys. I have been thinking, perhaps the best thing you could do would be to fail and fail and fail at everything you do, and then you will always be sent on new courses, and might last out the rest of the war without ever getting fully trained for anything, so that you would never ever be worth sending abroad. It is rather exciting about Tunis and Bizerta, isn't it, and filled me temporarily with vague hopes. The Germans, in this case, really having 'suddenly packed up'. When everybody (even Philip Gribble)[233] was still saying that they were still 'a tough nut to crack'. And now the Russians attacking all along the front.

I wonder if you've motor bicycled yet? How long is the motor bicycling part? Risk failing sooner than having accidents, won't you?

Fondest love, darling Heywood,

ANNE

From HEYWOOD   Wentworth Woodhouse

Tuesday, 11 May

From HEYWOOD

Darling,

I've just rung up and got on to Peta, who told me your pains had begun and you left this morning, so I am in a fever about you. *A*

---

233 A cousin of Heywood, who distinguished himself in the First World War in the Royal Flying Corps, precursor of the RAF; and led a colourful life after it, with several wives, fortunes made and lost, and finally dying at eighty-eight.

fever. I'm in the YMCA, and I've spilt the tea, and I can't really write to you because I go off into frenzies.

It sounded as if it were going to be a long confinement. Peta said how wonderfully *calm* you were. Mummy wrote me a letter about how wonderful you were. How wonderful to have gone on with the shop and all.

And then there's another fever case. I was sent for by the mobilisation officer tonight, and was told the plot[234] people want me for something or other, and would I like to try it.

He seemed rather to want me to stay. I said I did want it – so he said I would be sent off in 4 or 5 days. But I don't know where. I at once went to ask about leave, but they *won't* let me see the CO till Thursday. Maddening. So if I'll get any leave at all, God knows. *Perhaps* this weekend. Of course they very likely won't let me come – as it's all the same sort of thing over again as that Larkhill 48 hours. They'll say I must stay to have my kit and my balls inspected.

How, how are you and what *is* happening to you?

H

[Telegram to Heywood 12 May]
Anne had a daughter this morning everything all right will wire again this evening love Mama.

[Telegram to Heywood 12 May]
Darling Heywood feeling tremendously well Harriet is as we thought huge hearty hockey-playing Roedean girl am longing to see you wonderful about your move love Anne.

[Telegram to Anne at Princess Christian Nursing Home, 12 Clarence Road, Windsor, 13 May]
See you this evening deep love to you and Harriet wonderful Heywood.

Brian Reade, in a letter written in 1985, recalled: 'I remember writing and receiving letters at the time of Harriet's birth, and how he

234 Photographic Interpretation London.

suppressed his anxiety (though not from me) in order to cope with the awful motor-bike instructors.'

Heywood was given four days' leave, Thursday, 13 May to Monday, 17 May.

From ANNE   Windsor
                                               Tuesday, 18 May
Darling Heywood,

Everything goes on the same. Harriet has gained another oz., her complexion has cleared a good deal[235] and she feeds better and sleeps less at every feed.

I slept rather badly. Discovered at about 11 I could hear unmistakably Harriet crying from upstairs. I could only just hear it by taking my ears from inside the bedclothes, and of course couldn't resist every few minutes having a listen to hear if she still was. Then when that stopped after a bit there were several warnings and all clears – no gun fire, but it gave one a fright and a jump each time. Then about 4 there were fearful moans and groans of labour pains from along the passage – I later discovered that it was that poor woman who started last Thursday, and the doctor doesn't expect her to have it till tomorrow or next day. She is called Mrs Wipes. Then at 6 fed Harriet for about three quarters of an hour, then went to sleep and had an appalling nightmare about dreadful mad people. However, I feel perfectly well now.

No other very thrilling letters – quite a lot tiresome to answer, like Miss Cocke. Angela and Janetta are coming to see me on Friday

My letters from here will be ready for you – never mind.

It was wonderful seeing you for so long. Thank God you're not motor bicycling now.

                                     Fondest love from
                                               ANNE

From HEYWOOD   On the Windsor-London train
                                               Monday, 17 May
My dear Mummy,

I've just left Anne and am in the train for London. I catch one

235 Harriet was born with a bright pink rash over most of her face. To cure it gentian violet was applied, which changed the pink to navy blue.

down to Rotherham about 4 o'clock. They are both very well and Harriet has put on 2 ozs. Anne is able to feed her all right, though it takes a long time. It is very endearing, though I can't say she's a great beauty. Lots of hair – blue eyes – flat squishy nose – large mouth – tiny furious face. They've got a nice room on the ground floor looking on to the garden. I met the doctor – who is full of charm – he's going to make Anne stay in bed for 17 days, which is a good thing. I do hope you'll manage to get over to see her.

I had lunch with Mama most days, who was full of tact and kept away from the home while I was there – though I think she could hardly bear to. She's enjoying staying with the Crawleys[236] in the Castle. I went to the house one day, which is in the cloisters and old and pretty.

It was quite easy getting out and in from Peta's by bus. She has been immensely kind having us all to stay for so long, and has made it all much nicer and easier.

What with the baby and the fine weather and all, it has been a v.g. serene and wonderful four days.

I shall come back to earth with a bump tonight, but the idea of the move makes it not so bad.

I don't think it's worth your writing till I tell you what they are going to do with me.

The lunch was great fun.

Love

HEYWOOD

From HEYWOOD

London/Rotherham train
Monday, 17 May

Darling,

I rather believe that Reade was a grandson of Wynwood Reade,[237] so I wish I'd finished that book on *Martyrdom of Man*. But I'm not sure.

I put on a thin vest at Warwick Av. And am now very hot on the sunny side in this Rotherham train. It's one of those uncomfortable

236 Canon Crawley, chaplain to King George VI, was a cousin of Anne's mother.
237 Heywood was right. According to the *DNB*, William Wynwood Reade (1838–75), a traveller, novelist, controversialist and a special correspondent in the Ashanti War (1873), was nephew of Charles Reade (1814–84), author of *The Cloister and the Hearth* (1861). William Wynwood wrote against Roman Catholicism and other forms of religion.

compartments too. Everybody is sweating. Even the Wren opposite, who is upper class but a private. She's got a gold wrist-watch and an expensive ring. She's trying to read an Oscar Wilde omnibus, but she's finished *The Importance of Being Ernest* and she's stuck. She has to keep blowing soot from the pages. It's bound in Moroccoette.

I'm longing to start on the hard-boiled egg, but it's too early. We've just stopped at Melton Mowbray. Mrs Sternson was tremendously smart and hair just done. Ready for the river trip, I presume. It will all blow down unless she has a firm net. There was not time to think of going to the shop. I met Mr Smith and Jimmy in the street.

I have most truthfully seen from the window a white nun sitting in a meadow. Children playing around. Perhaps something holy is happening to me. You and Harriet in that room were like some annunciation.

Love dear,

H

From HEYWOOD   Wentworth Woodhouse
Tuesday, 18 May

Darling,

It wasn't too bad getting back though it's always nasty. There was another bus strike at Rotherham. (I took Trollope's *An Autobiography*. He married a Rotherham girl at Rotherham, I read.) There was a taxi with 5 others going back, and I squeezed in; but I lost a paper carrier with vests and Trollope and hanks, and a note I'd written to you. There's a faint chance I left it on the station.[238] Got back about 9. My bed taken in Corunna, but I found one in Peninsula – then a great job to find someone to undo the storeroom for my blankets and kit. I didn't get them till lights out, so had to grope about on a difficult top bunk, among the snores and farts. This morning I was told to parade for biking, so put on my crash helmet and goggles and went to a lecture on the machine. When I asked the sergeant what to do after that, he said report to Corporal Lead of the workshop, so I reported and was told to scrape mud off a broken bike. I kneel on the workshop floor and do it as slowly as I can, so they won't have to think of anything else for me to do. Occasional unintelligible quips are thrown at me, and I smile foolishly.

238 He had. It's the preceding letter (17 May).

Several enquiries about the baby from Duke and Schonsberg and Albert and the others. I seem to make friends easier here than in most places. Schonsberg had run into a wall on his bike, but survived. I can think of you very vividly, sitting in that room and Harriet going to sleep at the breast.

I find I have quite genuine strong feelings about Harriet. But maybe they won't last in the right way – once we get all squashed up together. I pray we may.

I thought I was present at some wonderful holy scene those four days.

Love

H

On the evening of Tuesday, 18 May, Heywood rang up to say he'd just been told that, despite all, he'd got the Photographic Interpretation job, and was to move to London the next day.

From HEYWOOD   In train, Rotherham/London
                                Wednesday, 19 May

Darling,

Now I'm in the train going back. Extraordinary, isn't it? Harris is with me – the punctilious man with a bald head who was at Matlock. I thought he'd gone, but he'd been on a week's leave. We've got to report to mysterious APIS this afternoon. He's been there before. Says it's 9 till 6.30 including Saturdays, and it's at Hammersmith (don't say so). He thinks they'll let me sleep at Warwick Av. I feel nervous about it. He says the OC has a bad temper. Nobody knows I'm coming up. Neither the Sternsons or Nancy. I mean to dump things at the shop on the way to Hammersmith. Hope I'll be ringing you up tonight.

Love

H

From HEYWOOD   10 Warwick Avenue
                                19 May, evening

Darling,

Harris and I took a taxi to the shop, where I dumped my things.

Mrs K. was there, who made some tea, and Harris washed. Then I helped Harris carry his things to the underground, and we went to Barons Court and St Paul's School, which was where we had to report. An AT told us to come back at 4.30, as Sergeant Jones was out, so we went to Hammersmith Bridge and sat by the river. At 4.30 Sergeant Jones was in the NAAFI, but after 5 he appeared, and we had to go and be signed in. He gave Harris a billet in Edith Road and said I could go home and report back at 8.30 tomorrow. So I went to the shop at just shutting time and rang you up, and Mollie and Nancy left and I lay in a coma fairly bewildered. I took a taxi to here and still no one was in but I climbed through the window as easy as anything. Then little Marlene came in like a poor little Cinders, and I tried to be nice for not long enough. Then I went to Norway and there she was talking to a policeman.

'They vere coddling in my doorvay,' she was bellowing – then she saw me and charged on me snorting – but had to go back to the policeman, who was stunned. 'No, I will not have it. Not in my house please.' The policeman left. There was one other poor woman there. 'Mrs Weiss, I ask Mr Hill. If Mrs Weiss's daughter was coddling in your doorway? I ask. Come, Mrs Weiss, stand up, I show you.' Mrs Weiss who is weak and small stood up, and Norway put her leg in her crutch and smothered her. Then Nancy came. 'No, Mrs Rodd. I do not have coddling in my house.' 'Oh – you are a spoilsport,' Nancy said. I couldn't help giggling by then. Lots about you and Harriet there was. She said she'd seen it in the *Evening Standard* which is odd.

The Sternsons have just come in from a cricket match – very blooming.

I'm frightened of my new school tomorrow and what they'll make me do. It's difficult to remember I must go there, as it feels so much like being on leave.

Love
H

From ANNE   Windsor
                                               Thursday, 20 May
Darling Heywood,

How wonderful and amazing to think of you at Warwick Avenue – though very tantalising I must say, my not being there. I long to hear about it. I'm so terrified it will be only for a fortnight or only 5 weeks, so that either we shall have no time at all together, or all the time we do have Sister Firth[239] will be with us. I am coming home on Tuesday week; start to get up tomorrow week. Am being given exercises to do, so hope I shan't be too weak.

Harriet was tremendously sick after her 6 o'clock feed this morning. I should think nearly a pint of milk shot out about a foot, sopping sheets, blankets, pillows, night-dress. She didn't seem to mind at all or cry, but didn't seem to want to start all over again afterwards. In spite of that she's again gained an oz. And now there's a theory she may be having too much to eat.

Shan't be seeing Mama today as it's her Mrs Wentworth[240] lunch day.

Feeling particularly well. My stitches are out (which made me sweat with fear and terror, but didn't really hurt badly at all).

Fondest love

ANNE

From HEYWOOD   10 Warwick Avenue
                                     Friday, 21 May

Darling Anne,

Today was my second day's work. I find it very exhausting – but expect that's the change and I'll get used to it. One has to be desperately neat, and one little blot or mistake is dreadful, as one is mostly plotting on a linen trace which other people have plotted on.

As always – the difficulty is to find exactly how and what one has got to do. Harris was vaguely told to tell me and he did quite a lot, but one doesn't really find out till one starts actually doing the thing. I sit next to a corporal who is self-important and officious, and tells me not to go to the NAAFI without telling the sergeant, and never to leave the cork out of the ink bottle, and so on. They are a clerky lot and a great deal of bad badinage goes on.

It's awfully odd how one is. Instead of the jubilation I ought to be in, I feel apathetic and stagnant. Maybe the heat. I can't bother to contact people, though I have met Moragh in the street and he's coming in tonight. He's already late and will prevent me going to

239 The monthly nurse.
240 Mrs Vernon Wentworth was a Suffolk neighbour and friend of Anne's mother.

bed early to get to sleep before the siren,[241] which I did beautifully last night and heard nothing. The first night I was frightened. Last night I had dinner at the British Restaurant – our one – and was allowed in in uniform. Tonight I went to the YMCA in Westminster, because I had to go near there with my cig. and choc. coupons. Both mornings I've left here too late and have had to take taxis to Olympia. Shocking.

Mr Sternson has absolutely stuffed veg. into the front garden. I'm certain it's all too crowded and close. He's planted peas where the beans were and is going to put tomatoes in front of them. It was Ross's birthday today. I hear Mrs S. singing 'Happy Birthday to You' at him this morning. As I came in tonight streams of smartly dressed dainty girls poured out. It was Ross's party but must have been mostly Marlene's.

There was a weatherbeaten (or perhaps careworn) woman there with a baby like a huge puffball. They were all thoroughly worn out by the party. The puffball had to be pushed to Chalk Farm in a sort of Rolls-Royce pram with a fur rug.

Don't repeat to *anyone* any of my complaints or job grumbles. It might so easily get back to someone and I'd be hurled back to hell.

Love
H

From HEYWOOD   10 Warwick Avenue
                                         Monday, 24 May

Darling Anne,

Mrs Sternson has gone off today till Friday on her hol. She's still determined to come to see you. Probably Saturday.

I worked very slowly at the plots today and didn't manage to say a word to anyone. I believe they are moving to Holland Park on Sat. I'm dining with Malcolm [Bullock] at his inevitable old Allies Club. Nancy says they have nothing but spam there. Wonderful to think you'll be here this time next week. I find I do have tender feelings for Harriet.

Love
H

241 At that time there was an air-raid warning at more or less the same time every evening. This continued for some weeks or even months. Usually nothing happened.

Postscript

Heywood went on doing Photographic Interpretation for the rest of the war, in various places. He was made a corporal on his transfer.

When I left the shop I had wanted and expected to work in it again, as before; probably, I'd thought, within a few weeks. But after having the baby I increasingly found that I didn't want to after all, which gave me the idea that perhaps I was not as indispensable as I'd imagined, and that if I worked part time only, and mostly at home, it might be enough. This proved to be the case, so I didn't go back ever (except very occasionally part time), and therefore, with Mrs Sternson's help, was able to look after Harriet myself. She didn't have to be a nanny after all, though (while she remained with me) she helped me in countless ways.[242]

No one in the shop was called up, and Nancy managed admirably without my being there fussing, as did Mollie and Mrs Kentall. I realise on reading the letters that I was far too emotional and possessive about the shop, which must have been maddening for Nancy. Though it meant considerably more work, she was, I should say, on balance much better off after I'd gone, when she was at last able to do things as she wanted in her own way. Certainly my many misgivings and fears turned out to be quite unfounded; and if I'd been 'in charge' without her, though the shop would probably have survived, I believe I would have done shockingly in comparison (particularly as I would have been wanting to hurry back to Harriet all the time).

When we first started in Curzon Street, Handasyde ('Handy') Buchanan was working in another antiquarian bookshop in the same street, Michael Williams, which was bombed in 1940. We got to know one another a little (though not well) in the four years before the bombing. We sometimes sent one another customers

242 After the war the Sternsons started a dry-cleaning business in Curzon Street and became highly successful.

(and also sometimes took them from one another). Heywood perceived that he was a knowledgeable and experienced bookseller, as well as a good salesman; so he wrote to him some time in 1944 asking whether, when the war was over, he might care to try working at No. 10. Handy agreed and was able to start in June 1945.

Soon after Handy's arrival Heywood got a letter from Nancy, saying that she had been given some money to start a business with. 'Do you want any money, would you like to have me as a partner?' she asked. Heywood said yes, he would, and she became one, for about twenty years.

In the same letter she said 'I can't work full-time any more, but could probably do three days a week, or every morning, or afternoon, as fits in best with the arrangements of others.' She was correcting the proofs of *The Pursuit of Love*, which came out in the autumn. Its great success enabled her to leave the shop altogether in March 1946, and in April she went to Paris, where she lived on the earnings from her books for the rest of her life.

Heywood went to stay with her nine months after her departure, and many times in the ensuing years. They collaborated in buying French books for the shop. They also kept up an increasingly frequent exchange of letters that ended only with her death.

At the end of April 1946 Elizabeth (Liz) Forbes came to work in the shop, and a few days later, on 1 May, Heywood was at long last demobilised. By this time Handy had been acting as manager during Nancy's absences for nearly a year.

So Heywood came back from the Army to a different, smaller shop, with three people in it he had never worked with before and knew only slightly or not at all. All of them were to stay till the mid-70s. A new era had begun.

In 1949 Handy and Mollie got married. In 1965 Heywood sold the shop to Henry Vyner, who re-sold it six years later to David Bacon. Heywood worked part-time till 1966, when, thirty years after first opening the shop, we both retired to Suffolk.

John Saumarez Smith had come to work in it about a year before Heywood's departure. On Handy's retirement in 1974 (ten years before his death), John replaced him as manager. He had by then become a friend, which formed a happy finale to our bookshop lives.

ANNE HILL

Biographical Appendix

Cranbrook, Dorothy, Dowager Countess of (1879-1968). Anne's mother, widow of the 3rd Earl of Cranbrook. Lived at Snape Priory near Saxmundham in Suffolk. Often referred to as Ma or Mama.

Cranbrook, John David, 4th Earl of (1900-78). The eldest of Anne's four brothers. At this time lived in the White House Farm, near Great Glemham in Suffolk. Called Jock. Married to **Fidelity** (b. 1912), daughter of Hugh Seebohm. Two sons and three daughters. Fidelity was a second cousin of Heywood.

Culme-Seymour, Angela. See Janet Woolley.

Frieze-Green, Mollie, *née* Catleugh, was introduced into the shop by Ruth Gathorne-Hardy and Sheila Hill (see below) soon after Heywood was called up.

Gathorne-Hardy, Antony (1907-76). Anne's youngest brother, a doctor who joined the Navy in 1939, where he remained after the war. Married to **Ruth** (1909-73), daughter of Commander Arthur Thorowgood. Two sons and a daughter: **Jonathan** (Jonny b. 1933), **Samuel** (Sammy b. 1936) and **Rose** (b. 1946). Ruth and her family spent the war first with Heywood's sister Sheila (see below) from 1940 to 1943, and after that with Fidelity and Jock Cranbrook.

Gathorne-Hardy, Edward (Eddie (1901-78). Anne's second brother. After leaving Oxford he worked for ten years in the antiquarian bookshop Elkin Mathews. He spent the war with the British Council in Athens and Cyprus and later Cairo, where he transferred to the Diplomatic Service.

Gathorne-Hardy, Robert (Bob) (1902-73). A writer and Anne's third brother. Before the war he too had worked in Elkin Mathews bookshop for a year. An early arm injury prevented him joining up, but he served in the Fire Service and later worked repairing bombed houses.

Griffin, Hester. The author of a number of novels and biographies written under the name Hester Chapman. She several times helped out in the shop at Christmas. Married to the banker **Ronald Griffin.**

Harrisson, Bridget (Biddy). Sister of Hester. Married first to Michael Clayton, then to **Tom Harrisson**, the anthropologist, writer and co-founder of Mass Observation.

Hill, Derek (b. 1918). Younger brother of John Hill (see below). Artist and writer.

Hill, George (1870-1961). Heywood's father. At this time recently retired from the Stock Exchange, he was in charge of the local Home Guard at Bignor, Petwoth, Sussex. Married to **Grace Johnstone** (1879-1959). They were referred to as Pa and Mother, or as the Orchards (from their house Great Orchard in Sussex) to lessen the confusion explained below.

Hill, John (1905-88). No relation to Heywood, an artist and interior decorator who ran a shop called Green and Abbott in St George's Street, London. He served in the RAF during the war, and was married to **Sheila Hill**, Heywood's younger sister. By 1942 they had three children: **Josephine** (Jo b. 1932); **Nicolas** (Nic) (b. 1934); and **Heywood** (b. 1941). In 1944 they had a third son, **Roderick** (Rod). John's parents were called the Sparsholts, after the village in Hampshire where they lived, to distinguish them from the Orchards.

Kentall, Mrs (Mrs K.) had worked in the shop as a cleaner before the war. She came back in 1943 and collected, packed and delivered books for the rest of the war.

Lambe, Charles. In 1942-3 he was a captain in the Navy working as Director of Plans in the War Cabinet. Later became Admiral of the Fleet and First Sea Lord. He was known in the Navy as the Red Admiral because of his liberal views. Married to **Peta**, a very old friend of Heywood.

Reade, Brian. The only person Heywood met in the Army who became a life-long friend. In 1941 he married the artist **Margaret Ware**. He had joined the Victoria and Albert Museum, working in the Department of Prints and Drawings. He returned after the war and in 1958 became Deputy Keeper. Author of a number of books: including on Edward Lear, Louis Wain, Beardsley (he organised the Beardsley exhibition at the V & A) and Spanish sixteenth-century costume.

Sinclair-Loutit, Janetta. See **Janet Woolley**.

Sternson, Mr and Mrs. They lived in Heywood and Anne's basement at 10 Warwick Avenue with their two young children, **Marlene** and **Rossie**. Mr Sternson was a wartime policeman; Mrs Sternson was what was then called a 'cook-housekeeper' to Anne.

Woolley, Janet (usually called **Jan**). The mother of **Mark** and **Angela Culme-Seymour**, and of **Janetta** and **Rollo Woolley**. All of them were connections of Anne's by marriage.

Index of Persons Named

*See Appendix